RAINCOAST
CHRONICLES

THIRTEEN

EDITED BY
HOWARD WHITE

HARBOUR PUBLISHING

RAINCOAST CHRONICLES 13
Copyright © 1991 by Harbour Publishing

Published by
HARBOUR PUBLISHING
Box 219
Madeira Park, BC Canada V0N 2H0

Editorial Assistant: Bryan Carson
Design and Cover: Gaye Hammond
Photographs and Illustrations:
   Front cover courtesy Helen Dawe; Back cover courtesy Gertie Lambert; 5, 6, 7, 8, 9 courtesy Florence Tickner; 10, 12 photos by Julia Moe; 14, 17, 19, 20 photos by Stephen Osborne; 22, 23, 24, 25 courtedy N.W. Emmott; 27, 29 courtesy BC Archives & Records Service (HP94613, HP2652); 31 photo by Liv Kennedy; 32, 33, 34 photos by Dan Propp; 36-37 photo by Stephen Osborne; 41, 42, 43, 44 courtesy Gertie Lambert; 45 courtesy BC Archives & Records Service; 46, 48, 49 photos by Bryan Carson; 50, 52 photos by Stephen Osborne; 58, 60,61, 62, 63 courtesy Paula Wild; 64, 66 courtesy Maurice McGregor; 69 photo by Philip Tims; 70, 71, 72, 73 courtesy Helen Dawe; 74 photo by Julia Moe.
   Illustrations on pages 38-40, 47, 54-55, 67, 75 by Gaye Hammond; 56 by Diana Durrand.
   Maps on pages 11, 59 by Gaye Hammond.
Printed and bound in Canada

CANADIAN CATALOGUING IN PUBLICATION DATA

Main entry under title:

Raincoast chronicles 13

   ISBN 1-55017-052-X

   1. Pacific Coast (B.C.) – History.   2. Pacific
Coast (B.C.) – Social life and customs.   I. White,
Howard, 1945–
FC3803.R34 1991   971.1'1   C91-091558-X
F1087.5.R34 1991

CONTENTS

The FLOAT HOUSE

FLORENCE TICKNER

IN THE EARLY DAYS up the coast very few permanent homes had been established on land. There were a few pre-emptions—the Hallidays at the head of Kingcome Inlet were the earliest in that area—a couple of small settlements, and the canneries. The logging camps were on floats, so they could be moved from place to place for easier access to the timber.

The floats were made of cedar logs, because they floated highest in the water. A smaller log was pulled onto each end and the logs were lashed to it. A float might last twenty or twenty-five years if it was made of good logs; some floats lasted even longer if they were tied up close to fresh water, so mussels or barnacles didn't grow. When the float started to sink too low in the water it was time to take drastic action. One or two logs were hauled crosswise under the float, in an effort to hold it up a year or two longer. This was done using the donkey engine. If the camp had to be towed to a new location, sometimes the logs rolled back out again; then it was time to start saving some new logs to build another float.

We always maintained that Uncle Earl Broyles logged in Thompson Sound in latter years, at the head of the inlet, because it was the only place the camp would stay afloat. The floats were almost sinking, but the abundance of fresh water kept the weed and barnacle growth down, and he was tied up in shallow water, with some extra logs pulled under the floats that probably touched bottom at low tide. Those floats were really old—some came from Moore's camp, and would date back to before 1910. In the fifties, Uncle Earl sold his camp and moved back to the United States. I feel sure the new owners wasted no time in putting together some new floats.

A logging camp might consist of from six to twenty floats, with a number of different buildings and/or equipment on them. The owner would have a house, and perhaps another house or two would be occupied by families. Many camps had a cookhouse, one or two bunkhouses, a wash house, a store house, a filing shed, a blacksmith shop and a tool house or shed. If you were on the shore side of the camp, you would see five or

Raising an A-frame in False Creek.

six outhouses strung along the back of the floats. Beside the buildings, the camp probably had a wood float – for fuel, a donkey float, a winch float, a drag-saw float, and maybe even an oil float. The more permanent floats were strung out in a line, and the donkey, wood, oil, drag-saw and winch floats were positioned where needed.

Many houses and other buildings were on skids, just sitting on floats, but some were decked in with planking. Some even had fences around them, to keep small children away from the water. We had a nice fenced-in area on one side of our house; Mother even had some plants in big tubs. I remember the "Snow on the Mountain" and honeysuckle. I planted the adipose fins from a big salmon in the honeysuckle tub when I was three or four, hoping to grow more salmon.

Our house was very small. It consisted of a lean-to bedroom and one large room, which was living room, dining room and kitchen combined. There was also a pantry, used for storing dishes and cooking supplies, with a sink at the end, and a window over it. There was no running water for the sink, but it drained into the salt water. When I was around four years old, Dad added a bedroom to the other side of the house, big enough for a double bed and a single bed, plus a small wood heater. This addition also had a closet, with drawers at the bottom. Before this, a small closet and chest of drawers in the lean-to was our only storage space for clothes. This doesn't seem like much room, but most of the clothes we had were either being worn or they were in the wash.

We also had another float with a shed on it, where our groceries, tools, etc. were stored. It was our meat house, too. Deer and ducks hung there when Dad had good luck hunting. We often played in the shed in poor weather, to get out from under Mom's feet. Usually there were clothes hanging in there, too; we had an outside clothesline, but in poor weather the shed came in very handy. It was also our spare bedroom.

Our cookstove had a warming oven above, and a water reservoir on the side. It was kept going all day, and provided heat for the whole house, except for the cold winter days, when the heater in the bedroom would be lit also. These stoves kept my dad busy at least one Sunday a month, cutting wood. The house wasn't insulated, although it was finished on the inside with v-joint, so you can realize it took plenty of wood to keep it warm. We children, especially my brother Ted and I, helped a lot stacking wood and cutting kindling. As we grew older, we were able to help out more and more in this respect. (I still have a couple of scars to show for early efforts with the axe.)

The back door was the "main entrance" to our house. The wood was stacked on the back porch, and the rain barrel was at the end. There were clotheslines strung there, too. We were supposed to keep the wood box in the house full, and the water tank on the stove topped up, but like most children, we usually had to be reminded. That little house, with its lack of space, comfort, style, or any modern conveniences, was a loving home to us, and we wished for no other.

Out the Window

FLORENCE TICKNER

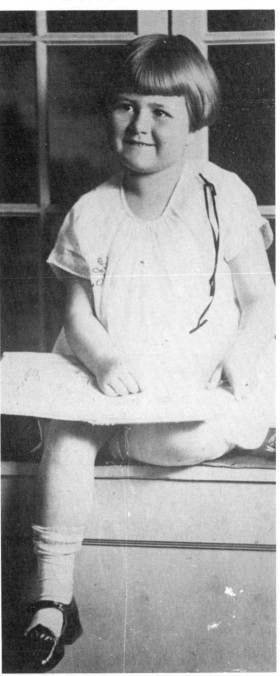

Florence Kimball (Tickner) as a young girl. This picture was taken when she was in Vancouver to have her tonsils out.

MOTHER AND DAD were both good swimmers and they encouraged us to learn as soon as we were able. Every year or so we would hear of someone who had drowned, and they certainly didn't want it to happen in our family. When we were playing outside we often fell in, sometimes just getting our feet wet, but occasionally going in right over our heads. Mom told the story of a time before I remember, of me falling in, and Ted watching me in the water. He didn't holler or anything; in fact it was the quiet that brought Mother out to investigate. There I was, slowly sinking in the water, and she just managed to grab me by the hair. No wonder they taught us to swim early!

Grandma Moore and her sister Alice never learned to swim. Perhaps it was because they were old-fashioned and modest, but never to my knowledge did they even try. They were certainly different in their reactions in the water, too. Grandma Moore fell in once or twice, which was inevitable, but it presented very little problem, because she floated. Aunt Alice, on the other hand, was a sinker. Dad told of the time Aunt Alice fell in and sank right to the bottom. There was no one around, but luckily she knew the direction to shore, and calmly walked that way until her head came out of the water. It was very fortunate that the water wasn't too deep.

7

Florence, Ted, Barbara and Shirley Kimball, in for a swim. The building on the left is a storage shack.

From the twenty-fourth of May until early in September we were in the water almost every day, and usually our bathing suits didn't have time to dry. It's a wonder we didn't grow fins. I learned to swim before I was six, so didn't miss out very much in the fun, because the others weren't as fast to learn. That first summer I practised every day, swam longer and longer distances, and by the time fall came Mother didn't have to worry about me.

On Sundays the swimming sometimes took a different turn. We had races, and the folks helped us with diving. We started out jumping, then graduated to "seal diving." That's kneeling down and sort of rolling in, making as little splash as possible. One Sunday, when

Dot Botta, Ada Willett, Vera Moore and Peter Botta in an old rowboat. Note the bowl haircut.

I hadn't been swimming very long, Dad lifted me up in his arms, and threw me out into the water as far as he could. That was a real shock, and I was really out of breath when I came to the surface. It was good practice, though, for when you fell in unexpectedly.

One of the things we used to do was see how deep we could go in the water. Sometimes we were tied up where you could see bottom, so then we would dive in, swim to the bottom, and bring back some sand or rock to prove we had made it. One very important thing I learned was that if you drop a rock underwater, it makes a terrible noise when it hits bottom. No wonder it is so easy to scare fish.

Living in float houses, and in isolation, there really wasn't much devilment we could get into. Besides that, our father was pretty strict, and we were careful not to stretch his patience too far. But the summer before our private teacher arrived, we three girls had some fun that I'm sure neither Mom nor Dad knew anything about. We had acquired a one-room house from Dad's folks, and Shirley, Barbara and I slept there before the teacher moved in. The door could be seen from the house, but there was a window in the back, and we used that to climb in and out, when we were skinny-dipping at night! Oh, what a wonderful sensation—the water was like velvet on our skins.

THE SINKING
OF THE
Arlene P

JULIA MOE

"FAN-TAN, FAN-TAN, FAN-TAN," a tense voice came over the scratchy marine radio speaker. The code book lists the call as "pan, pan, pan, pan," for urgent problems like engine trouble in bad seas or water coming in faster than the pump can push it out, but I always hear it like a call from China sending out war news.

His voice was tense, but so calm. All through that afternoon I wondered at his lack of hysteria as we ran up and down the boardwalk, primed the fire pump, and pumped and gassed and positioned the inflatable fifteen-foot *Canova* for an instant launch. It looked so small and aged and fragile outlined against the huge waves running offshore, but at least it was there. Several times I caught myself on the edge of panic, but his voice was a steady rock through that storm.

"This is the *Arlene P*, we're off Lippy Point, just north of the entrance to Quatsino Sound, and we're

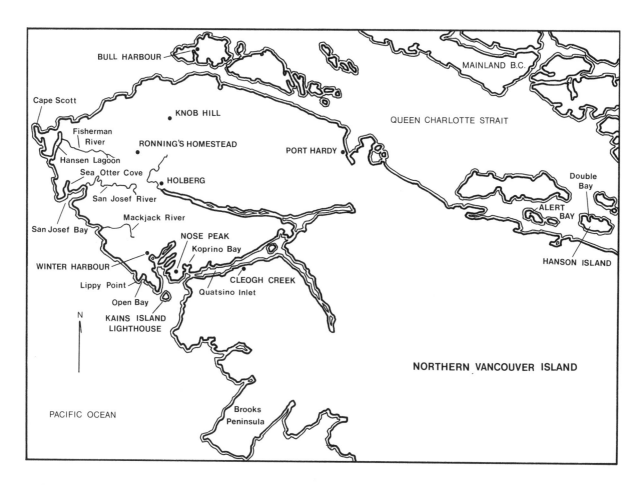

taking on water faster than we can pump it out. We still have power, but the water's rising in the engine room and the engine will go if we can't get help soon. Is there anyone around that could get a pump to us out here?"

"The *Arlene P*, the *Arlene P*, this is Alert Bay Coast Guard Radio. You are requesting a pump and not immediate rescue, is that correct?"

"Yes, we still have power, if someone can get a pump to us so we don't lose the engine, I think we can make it to Quatsino Sound."

"The *Arlene P*, can you give us a description of your boat, how many people aboard, and your exact location?"

"We're just off the mouth of Quatsino Inlet, Alert Bay. There's two of us, and we're a green-and-white gillnetter, thirty, thirty-one feet, green hull and grey and white, white cabin."

"The *Arlene P*, can you give a more exact location?"

"We're just going by Lippy Point right now, it's two miles north of the entrance to Quatsino Sound, Cape Parkins is ahead, the next point south, and then there's the turn to go into Winter Harbour."

"I can't quite make you out, the *Arlene P*. Is that Licky Point, I repeat, Licky Point? Can you give a longitude and latitude?"

"No, that's *Lippy* Point, *Lippy* Point, right off the west coast of Vancouver Island, south of Cape Scott, just before you turn into Winter Harbour. Can you get a pump to us right away or we'll be in real trouble?"

His voice made Lippy Point clear and emphatic, but it never turned shrill. Ron and I were both standing right next to the speaker by this time, and his last question made my stomach bottom out. "Oh, my God, look at the weather out there, Ron. I just gave 40 and gusting on the last weather report." Ron wasn't looking out the window, though. Still staring at the radio speaker, he said, "We've got the fire pump here. I'll get it ready; he's only about two miles away."

"This is Alert Bay Coast Guard Radio, is there anyone in the area of Quatsino Sound, anyone in the area of Quatsino Sound, that can come to the aid of a vessel in distress?"

Ron was riffling through the phone book. "If I can't get the pump out there, maybe somebody in Winter Harbour can." His finger was just moving down the opened page toward the Winter Harbour listing when the radio buzzed and crackled and spoke again.

"...eeker, I'm already on my way out from Winter...should...half an hour, maybe more, I don't know, though, it's looking kind of rough."

"This is Alert Bay Coast Guard Radio. You say you're on your way to the *Arlene P*? Can you repeat your name and position?"

"This is the *Little Streaker*. I'm on my way out from Winter Harbour, about halfway to the lighthouse, to Kains Island, and I think I can be there is half an hour if I can get past the island, but it's looking pretty windy."

It was pretty windy. The rock cut where we launch our boat was still protected, but the sea beyond was running strong: the *Canova* wouldn't make it far offshore. Ron was now down at the boat shed with the hand-held radio. I was standing by the lighthouse radio system in the house; we knew they'd want a current weather report from here and maybe contact for some other reason. As the *Little Streaker* came into view behind the island, I left the house and ran down the boardwalk to help Ron get the pump winched aboard the boat, a two-person job.

"*Little Streaker*, this is Kains Island," Ron said into the portable radio. "We've got a pump and can get it out to you as you go by if you can take time to stop for it."

"Kains Island, I can get it aboard here, but it's too rough out there, I won't be able to use it. All I can try is tow him in, if I can get out there."

By now the *Little Streaker* was slamming up and down on the steep, curling waves. She was only a foot longer than the small gillnetter already out there and probably a worse sea boat, being fiberglass, built light and shaped for speed, but with no steadiness for a high sea. She disappeared through the cut behind the island, and I shivered in the strong wind, though it was warm for January. Static crackled loud out of the tiny radio's speaker while we waited for another voice. The *Little Streaker* came back through the cut.

"*Arlene P*, this is the *Little Streaker*, I can't make it out behind the island, the sea's too big. I'll try around the front and now." The white bow edged out from the protection of the island and I ran back down the boardwalk to watch it from the house at the island's south end, where I should have been back at the radio anyway. Ron stayed with the boat ready to launch in case *Little Streaker* could tow the *Arlene P* this far and get the pump aboard in the lee of the island.

"*Little Streaker*, *Little Streaker*, can you bring us that pump? The water's to the bottom of the engine now; we don't have much time before we lose power."

The *Little Streaker* was wallowing up the inside of a foaming breaker, nose plunging through the arc, engine racing frantically as the prop skewed crazily out of the sea. Another one just as bad, and Harold used all twenty-three years of born-on-a-troller knowledge to make his last-chance turn and get surfed back into the lee of the island again.

"I can't make it past Kains Island. It's too rough for me to get out there."

"Is there anyone else that can get us a pump? I don't think we'll last long without our engine." That voice still held steady despite what he was saying. I looked at the chart on the wall. Just past Lippy Point, his only chance for shore was Open Bay, one sandy notch in that whole stretch of steep, rocky coast. Surely somebody somewhere somehow could get to him. That's

when a tug came on the radio, but from way up Quatsino Inlet, with a tow, two hours estimated running time to the *Arlene P.* and it couldn't get that close in to shore anyway with its towline. Surely someone, somewhere, somehow.

"The *Arlene P*, the *Arlene P*, this is Alert Bay Coast Guard Radio. There is a Buffalo aircraft on its way to you, departed from Comox fifteen minutes ago with an ETA to your position of half an hour. You should be able to see it in your vicinity in a short while."

"Alert Bay, Alert Bay, the water's in the engine now, it's starting to die, we're going to lose power. Does the plane have a pump?" That voice was smooth as a surf-washed rock while the erratic clangs and groans of the stalling engine racketed around it.

"Yes, the Buffalo has a pump and life rafts that he will drop to you. Give us the exact degrees of your location so that he can find you. Do you have any flares aboard?"

"Yes, we have flares. My partner's getting them out now." There was only radio static behind his voice now. "The engine just quit. We're getting into our dry suits now. Tell us when to set off a flare."

Out of the dark belly of clouds to the east appeared the yellow slit of the Buffalo Search and Rescue plane, small and bright against the dim hill behind and grey clouds above. It banked and started circling the edge of the hills around Quatsino Sound. No, no, it's not in here, out farther, go out farther.

"The aircraft is having trouble finding you, *Arlene P*. Set off a flare now. Can you see the aircraft? He should be on the radio any time now."

A roar of static came over the speaker with a small, faraway voice somewhere within. The Buffalo hadn't seen a flare; had the *Arlene P* set one off? Could it give a more exact location?

The *Little Streaker* broke in, "Buffalo Aircraft, just keep going straight out the direction you're headed now, go west, straight west, the *Arlene P* is outside Kains Island and the Cape."

"We see the plane, we see the plane. The first flare misfired. We're setting off another. Does he see us now?"

The yellow body of the plane disappeared over the Cape to the west, seeming to skim the tops off the trees. The trees themselves began to fade and disap-

pear from sight as the rain set in and the sky closed in thick.

"We see you, the *Arlene P*. We're circling once and on the second pass we'll drop the pump to you."

"We've lost power, Buffalo, so we can't get it unless you drop it close. We're getting ready to launch our life raft and try to pick it up with that."

"The pump is dropped, *Arlene P*. Can you retrieve it?"

"It's too far out, maybe with the skiff, wait, it might blow our way, yes, it's coming this way, maybe we can get hold of the line, no, wait, yes, yes, he's got it, we've got the pump, we've got the pump aboard." The voice broke off. I could picture the two fellows, frantic to make it work, trying to keep hands calm as they pulled and worked at the wrappings.

"The boat is sinking," came the voice from the Buffalo. "The two men are launching their raft." Silence again. "Their skiff has overturned; we've dropped another life raft. I can see one man hanging onto . . ." The voice cut off, and it never came on again. They must have switched from the marine emergency channel to their own aircraft connection to Alert Bay Radio.

By then it was almost dark and the rain so heavy we couldn't see more than half a mile into it anyway. We listened all evening for more news, and when Ron gave the late marine local weather report at 7:30, we asked the radio operator at Alert Bay what had happened. The last he'd heard, the Buffalo had dropped a life raft and a helicopter was now standing by in Port Hardy, but the visibility and darkness had kept it from trying a search today. It would have to wait for first light in the morning.

I couldn't tell the difference between my fears and dreams that night; it was all big waves and cold water and one man with his hand on the life raft and the other man not even there at all. Long before dawn we were staring at darkness through the eastern windows, door open so we would hear the first drone of the helicopter heading this way. Finally at eight we could stand it no longer and called Port Hardy to find out if the helicopter had left. It was just getting ready to leave, but the Buffalo had stayed out there circling into the night and last reported a fire on the beach at Open Bay and two men waving.

HOW I GOT THE DUMP JOB

HOWARD WHITE

A LOT OF OUTSIDERS, when they hear I work at the Blueband Bluff Sanitary Disposal Unit as Supervisor of Solid Waste, immediately offer their condolences and draw back, as if I had confessed to a terminal case of leprosy.

Egbert Rorscharch, one of my colleagues from the work poetry movement in Vancouver, came up to visit us one day while I was at the dump and Susan sent him over. I saw him drive into the compound in his VW van and signalled him to wait while I finished the bit of garbage cleanup I was working on.

The dump was on fire this day and I'd been pushing all the garbage up in a big holding pile so I could clear the one-acre dump site before tipping the pyramid of fresh trash into the flames. I did it this way because once the new garbage caught fire and Blueband Bluff's weekly accumulation of screw-top wine bottles started exploding it wasn't safe to be within a half mile of the place. If you saved that move until last, you could do it in a couple of fast swoops before the fire took hold and be out of the way before the glass really started flying, and this was what I had to do now.

This work poet was a town guy who wore a Mao-Tse-Tung hat and wrote about work more than he actually did it as far as I could see, so I thought he might enjoy watching me engaging the actual beast for a few minutes. The trouble was, I'd pushed up this small mountain of old fridges, broken sofas, dog-smelling carpets and carcasses of poached deer about the size of the Blueband Bluff Community Hall a bit too close to the flames and the new garbage was starting to light up before I got out of it, and my lungs were just about bursting.

The heavy artillery thuds of the wine bottles were starting up like the first kernels in a batch of popcorn. I knew I should leave it for the day, but I have never been much good against the temptation to finish up, at a little risk to life and limb. I went charging back into the fray with my hand over my nose, gearing down as the cat took up the weight of the tons of used Pampers, castoff stuffed toys, broken lawn furniture and crunching aerosol cans. By working fast I was able to keep a little more green garbage on the fire than it could quite light up in the time it took me to scoot back for another push. But the longer I went clattering back and forth, scraping up bucketloads of garbage bags that broke open leaving windrows of steak bones and coffee grounds, the hotter the main heap became, until critical mass was reached and the aerosol cans began shooting off, trailing smoke in all directions, and the whole glowing mountain started exploding like a kamikazed ammunition dump. There was more smoke too, but it was the safer inky-black stuff now and as the jagged neck of a two-litre Sommet Rouge bottle splashed against the metal guard behind my ear, a window opened in the murk and I saw Egbert running for cover. I thought he might be a little bit awed by the danger, action etc. of a real person performing this act his writings laboured to describe, but when I finally walked up to shake his hand, tears cutting tracks through the mask of soot on my face, he was shaking his head.

"Do you have to do this?" he said, half-accusingly. "Couldn't you make as much if you spent the same amount of time writing?"

Do you have to do this? I opened my mouth to explain, but the gulf between his background as a city doctor's son and mine as a gyppo logger's son was just too big for me to bridge at the moment, and my brain was still convulsing from the big dose of phosgene gas I'd taken in.

"Let's go have a beer," I croaked instead.

In the days before I got the dump job, I didn't go out for beer. The Roost was always full of guys sitting around drinking up their pogey cheques. They would never seem to notice my presence, but it wouldn't be long before I'd hear some artificially raised voice behind my back:

"Better watch yer language, I see we got the intelligentsia with us today."

"It's good to see our taxes going to a good cause."

"Yeah, for a change."

Back in the sixties when Keynesianism was still alive I'd gotten an Opportunities for Youth grant to employ seven young people taping oldtimers, and since then had turned that fledgling effort into a pretty respectable little book publishing company. But twenty years later local outrage showed no sign of dying down. It was nurtured by the editor of the local newspaper, who would give us a headline every time one of our poetry books got sixty percent of its deficit subsidized by the Canada Council.

I'll meet someone I went to school with in the liquor store where we can't avoid speaking, just after one of our books has had a three-page writeup in the front of *Maclean's* with colour, and this guy'll say "What are you doing these days?" Carefully. Not the offhand "Whatcheruptoo?" like they say to each other. They mostly know I fiddle around with books in some way, the way I've done forever, but see it as a sort of pretentious hobby that has kept me from ever getting down to business and earning an honest living like the Knockrust boys, who have good jobs running loaders at the gravel pit, or even Hippy John, who at least gets out cooking on Billy Solomon's seineboat every summer. Mrs. Quinlan, the star socialite who heads up the local pro-life and hanging movement, would sometimes offer me odd jobs when she met Susan in the crowded noon-hour post office, kitchy-kooing our little boy. "You poor wee thing you," she'd twitter.

The Cedardalers had had the dump job locked up for a long time. Cedardale is the next town down, a seaside shopping community that hasn't progressed an intellectual hair's breadth since Sinclair Lewis put the North American shopping town under glass in 1922 in *Babbitt*—which, interestingly, makes Cedardale seem very much in tune with the guiding lights of the 1990s.

Not the least of the resemblances between it and the Gopher Prairie Lewis wrote about is its conviction the people of the surrounding countryside were placed there by God to be bilked without let or hindrance. This process is greatly aided in Cedardale's case, as it is all over BC, by a super-municipal level of government known with redundant splendour as the Regional District.

We had started the Blueband Bluff dump ourselves, using volunteer help, in a skunk cabbage hollow behind the school, but when the Regional District came in, Cedardale got control of it, along with our one street light at the turnoff from the highway. We were leery of Cedardale getting a hold of our swamp-fed waterworks, but we couldn't see any harm in giving them our garbage. It was several years before we realized all the work in the dump was now being paid for with money from taxes, and all this money was going to Cedardale guys. This became a serious issue.

Every time the Regional District elections came up, the one issue all candidates would be required to embrace was "getting those bastards from down the road out of our garbage dump." Cedardale, with its majority on the board, would laugh off these periodic eruptions of the popular will and after thumping the table a bit about Cedardale making a travesty of the British Parliamentary system, our new delegate would settle down to the more absorbing business of divvying up junkets to places like Campbell River, Kamloops and Pouce Coupe.

Then Cedardale went too far. They announced they were closing the Blueband Bluff dump and thenceforth all garbage would be trucked twenty-five miles down the winding Raincoast Highway to the One Big Dump at Cedardale—in the name of efficiency. Well, Blueband Bluffers had swallowed the argument that the local dump had to be operated by Cedardalers because it would be inefficient to deal with a separate garbage contractor for each place, but when it came to hauling tons of sloshing garbage from one end of the Cook Peninsula to the other instead of just flopping it in a hole where it was made, they knew they were being had.

An outraged delegation led by me confronted the commissioner, a frog-faced paraplegic named Kurt Reimer who'd weathered more scandals than Tammany Hall, and he abruptly switched tactics and declared the Blueband Bluff dump had to be closed for sanitary reasons. When I demanded to know the sanitary reasons, he waved a two-year-old letter of complaint from the Department of the Environment at me and said it didn't matter, the decision was already made, and tomorrow we could start putting our garbage in neat little cans ready for roadside pickup. Our own delegate, a mystical, wild-talking stump-rancher famed for his proposals to build bridges over every lake and dead-end slough in the country, not to mention the Strait of Georgia, sided with his new junket-mates and told me I was out of my tree. Only he would have been sufficiently out of touch to make such a disastrous

miscalculation, because he threw his own garbage in the brush behind his house and didn't realize how important the dump had become to Blueband Bluff social life.

There is no community centre in Blueband Bluff. There's no town square. There are no shops to browse in. There is no ballpark, no racetrack. The dump is all we have.

I don't know what it is about the dump, really. All I know is, it's the heart and soul of the community. We tried to think up all sorts of excuses for it, and I tried to put them into words in my petitions and letters to the paper. I said, a place like this has a different garbage than little ticky-tacky imitation suburbs like Cedardale. We had a lot of old fridges, I said, and car bodies, and stumps. "Perhaps Mr. Reimer will be good enough to send us instructions for inserting a five-foot fir stump into a Glad bag," I tub-thumped. I kept wanting to say, "There's not a person in Blueband Bluff who doesn't spend some of their most contented moments picking over that dump, looking for treasures," but my political instincts told me to avoid that simple truth at all costs. Instead I wrote the Department of the Environment.

They wrote back and said their reason for wanting the dump closed was that it was always in such a mess, and the Regional Board had assured them the only solution to this was to close it, since they were too far away to look after it properly and no one in the area had shown any interest in taking on the job. I duly published this revelation in the paper, and the next day collected 400 signatures in two hours in the shopping centre parking lot. No one even knew there were 400 people in Blueband Bluff before. I called a meeting in the community hall which Reimer was fool enough to come to, and I wasn't halfway through my speech before the mob was too loud to be heard over. Reimer was lucky to escape alive, and if he'd been a healthy man he certainly wouldn't have escaped unbeaten. As it was, he reported to the Board later that he had been "denounced in the vilest language I've ever heard in my life."

The mystic stump-rancher now experienced a change of faith and came forward with a proposal that the dump be kept open and maintained by a local contractor to be chosen by public tender. His junket-mates solemnly consented, as though this was the solution they'd been looking for all along, and nothing to do with me. But they hadn't forgotten me. When I put in a bid on behalf of our family sand and gravel outfit and it turned out to be $96 a year lower than anyone else's, they awarded the contract once again to the Cedardale company, declaring the gravel in our pit was too coarse to make good cover material.

I immediately contacted the capital, and after some arguments and counter-arguments, a low-ranking official from the office of the undersecretary to the assistant deputy minister of intergovernmental affairs decided to come out and inspect our gravel pit to see if there was any substance to Reimer's low opinion of our

gravel. This was the most serious attention the Cook Peninsula had received from senior government in the memory of most people, and a kind of hush fell over the area.

It also left me in a rather awkward position. Reimer's assessment of our gravel was perfectly accurate. Blue-band Bluff is made out of good healthy granitic schist and has neither soil nor decent gravel. What we called our gravel pit was really just a hole in the hillside where the maker had cached about two thousand tons of leftover twelve-inch boulders, fixing them firmly in place with an interregnum the colour and consistency of neat Portland cement. But there were two serious flaws in Reimer's argument. One, it doesn't matter what the hell you use to cover up garbage. And two, I knew where there was one tiny isolated pocket of about ten truckloads of lily-white pea-gravel smooth enough to be used in a Japanese rock garden. If I could dig out that pea-gravel and pour it down over the boulders before the inspectors came to look, we'd get our dump back.

There was just one problem. To move the gravel I'd have to get the loader up the ten miles of highway to the pit, and to haul the loader I'd have to use our truck, which was broken down as usual. It was sitting on twelve-by-twelve blocks with both axles out, and the bogey was completely wrecked. The government men were coming in five days.

The first two days I spent telexing around western Canada and the US trying to find a heavy-duty junk-yard that had ever heard of a bogey as antique as ours. The next day I spent trying to persuade the other local truckers to give me a lift but they wouldn't touch me with forty feet of frozen tow rope. As far as they were concerned, antagonizing Reimer was foolish and med-dling with the feds was suicide.

That left me with Ole Stronghold. Ole was out working on a subdivision in my neighbourhood, and I'd been doing some hauling for him off and on. Whenever I worked there I'd start out doing something Ole told me, then one of his two partners would stop me and say "don't listen to that Stronghold, he's nuts — go over there." But then we'd all get together for lunch and spend two and a half hours listening to Ole's cockamamie analysis of the world monetary crisis (he predicted the fall in interest rates before anyone I know) and his plans for a big subdivision somewhere in the Caribbean, which we were all invited to work on.

Ole got all his news from the *National Enquirer* and read moving his lips, but he was one guy who kept up on what was going on. He couldn't get over the fact I made these books, and always made me tell him when I was going to be on TV or the radio so he could catch it. Then he'd want to know everything about the interviewer's private life, how I set the gig up, what the building looked like inside, until he couldn't think up anything more to ask. "Quite the deal, quite the deal, quite the deal," he'd say, shaking his head as if he couldn't believe what he was hearing.

Ole had been following my tussle with the dump and was highly amused.

"Do you really think you can lick those crooks?" he said.

"Donno. Guess I'll find out pretty quick now," I said, looking worried.

"Ha ha ha ha. Wellsir, if there's any way I can help, you just let me know. Hahha ha ha ha. You show 'em."

He was the first to offer his truck.

"You take that damn truck there!" he said.

It was an old cornbinder with a rockbox he'd just bought for $6,000, a ridiculous price for a tandem with diesel. I measured up the box and figured the cat would just barely fit. But the catch was, this truck didn't have a licence. In fact Ole had been nailed bringing it up the Peninsula in broad daylight and fined $2,800 just a week before. That was about what you'd clear with the dump contract in a year.

This was Saturday night. The untitled official from the undersecretary of the assistant deputy minister was coming Monday morning.

I stewed about it all that evening. One moment it seemed crazy. Going out in an unlicensed truck the cops were already on the lookout for was inviting certain disaster. I would be struggling along at 10 or 15 mph, overloaded beyond thinking, a sitting duck. Better just forget it. Forgetting it, my spirits rose as if I'd been carrying the cat myself. Then I thought of the official and all the board members standing in the pit looking at God's own boulder museum. No way would they pass that mess. I'd be left whining that boulders didn't matter, the loser again, more a pariah than ever, my kid doomed to a life of ridicule...the bulldozer was on my back again. Then suddenly it was off and I was soaring free again: I'd sneak down in the night, nip up to the pit in less than half an hour, zip back, bail out my pea-gravel, wow the government guy, win the contract, never look back. The chance of running into the cops at 4:00 a.m. Sunday was one in a million. Except if that hopeless overload snapped an axle and stranded me out there, big as a blimp in the bright sun...or what if the brakes gave out and I ploughed into a school bus carrying three basketball teams, with no insurance? When I finally fought myself to sleep at three, I still hadn't made up my mind.

I woke up at six and sat bolt upright in bed.

"What's wrong?" my wife said.

"I'm going," I said.

"Please don't." She put everything into it.

"I've gotta." I don't know who said it. The next thing I knew I was slamming the door, fly undone, boots untied, hair flying, gone.

This was March, so it wasn't quite light but it was well on the way. The air was raw and blue with wet chill, but not raining, a few lonely birds threeping in the trees. The truck hunched in the mud, covered with dew and cobwebs like a spectre-ship. I bolted the licence plates from our truck on, fore and aft.

The starter sounded like a cement-mixer. My heart sounded like a Sikorsky Sky-Crane. Maybe it wouldn't start, and I'd be free! I would have tried!

It started. It took fifteen minutes to get the air up enough to unlock the maxi brake, and the first time I punched the foot brake the air dropped thirty pounds. Practically no brakes at all. If I'd had five minutes I could have set up the back slack adjusters and got something, but I was already two hours behind schedule, and I was shaking too much to hang onto a nine-sixteenths spanner anyway. I pushed the clutch in, found low and crawled out of the mud, the totally foreign sensations of the truck filling me with panic at how little I knew it. No lights. I couldn't have started earlier anyway. No wipers. I tried to stick my head out the window. It banged the glass. The glass fell down with a crash. I reached outside and wiped a muddy hole in the windshield dew with my hand. I found third.

I pulled up to the loading ramp where my brother had left the cat, set the maxi, flowed out the door up onto the cat, started it, back down to block the truck and back up to the cat all in one hunched, blindly flailing motion as if acting it all out in a trance, realizing I'd been rehearsing every detail in my mind, hundreds of times, for the last twenty-four hours. I was somewhere far beyond myself, or beneath myself, in the grip of powers I knew not, could not question or control. And yet look how I tended to every detail, without a split second's hesitation. Somewhere a tape was running with all the right moves recorded on it. Like a completely detached observer I noted with approval how snugly the safety chains were set, and even remembered to snatch a rag and wipe the windshield before getting back in.

Then I was crawling up the hill in low under. You could walk faster. You could walk backwards.

It was roaring a feeble, muffled roar somewhere far behind, just hanging on at bottom revs. I'd felt more torque in a Volkswagen. Passing over a shallow dip, it heaved like a schooner in a squall—IT'S GOING OVER! No, not quite. All but. What a ride we're in for. It'll take all day. At that point the venture seemed pure suicide.

I bullied the old battle-weary, straight-cut gears into submission, gearing down at the bottoms of hills not to take a chance on missing a shift, stalling, and running away backwards with the useless brakes,

rolling the cat, wrecking the truck, flattening a house full of sleeping people, going to jail forever. Jail! If only I were there now, and not here! Gearing down to a crawl at the tops of hills...

Maybe I will come to my senses and pull into the old man's place before I actually hit the highway, I thought, picking up speed on the Rowboat Pass bridge, noticing all the scraping and flapping noises rising like a Martian orchestra tuning up behind me. Whap whap whap whapwhapwhap, squeak, squeak, wobble wobble-wobble. I wobbled past the old man's at a great rate.

Grinding up onto the highway, I realized for the first time it was now broad daylight. It was 7:10 a.m., and it had taken me twenty minutes to come the first three miles. It seemed twenty years.

The highway, stretching north of Blueband Bluff, lay before me like the rest of my life. At any moment I could visualize every curve, every dip, every hill that stood between me and salvation, all at once as if I were in a dirigible looking down, or in close-up magnifica-

tion so I could finalize my strategy for getting past each obstacle in the smallest detail. Going down the slopes alongside the lake I would get it in fifth over—if the pathetic old engine had the jam—and squeeze out every erg of acceleration I could get in readiness for the long pull up to the Roost. I'd get back into fourth by the end of the lake where the slight incline began, cheat on the curve by the turnoff—nobody awake yet anyway—then drop to third, second and second under in quick succession. She should hump it over the top in second under.

Second under wasn't enough. I had to go to low over, but I made the near-impossible split shift without a sound. But oh, I seemed to be pinned to that hillside forever, grinding and grinding but standing stock still, like a painted truck upon a painted road. I heard a car slide in behind me. My ears tensed for the burp of siren, my consciousness roaring in my ears like a waterfall, senses numb. I knew eternity then.

At the top of the hill the car, a harmless and listing Olds loaded with tousle-headed guys all arms and legs like crabs in a full crab pot, flapped past into the driving snow. Snow! Good Christ, a heavy snowstorm

had suddenly begun, of all things, on March 27. It comforted me actually, like a blanket. I didn't feel so exposed. In any case, I now had a long decline and I could ramble. Then I'd be at Misery Corner and well over halfway to heaven, with only an easy climb through Fall Meadows and a level stretch to the pit turnoff. My face stuck out the side window in the driving, stinging snow; every yard of safe progress came to me like an answered prayer. My nerves were all quivering in anticipation of the next problem—the hairpin turn at Misery Corner, seeing over and over a vision of the rig toppling into the deep ditch. But I'd check the road ahead for traffic while I was coming down the hill, then once I knew it was clear, I could cut right across the turn. It worked. I glided up out of the hairpin like I was riding on a ferris wheel.

Now just that mile-and-a-half pull to Fall Meadows, and we're home free. Again, pounding up the incline like a grade A turkey awaiting certain fate, again the blood-chilling swish of tires behind, again the prickly sensation in the scalp I imagined to be my hair turning white right there on the spot, like dry grass before a blaze; again reprieve. Then the top gained, the flapping banging clanging charge down the other side and sanctuary.

I crawled up the muddy side road in low low, not breathing free until the last slash of highway disappeared in trees. The pit was a half hour further into the bush but my much-rehearsed plan was to dump the cat at the first cut-bank I came to and hustle the truck back to Ole at the jobsite. In the brief reprieve of this shelter my senses returned enough to allow me to view this next plan as the most insane yet. After all, Ole would forgive me for stranding him without his truck for one day, and I could sneak it back at daybreak Monday. But again the tape was playing. I would be fast on the trip back without the load, then it would be all behind me, all over. In my confusion I almost dumped the truck on its side trying to get square to a bank that turned to mud, but miraculously freed myself and found a better unloading site.

Having got rid of the cat, I went crashing back down onto the highway and started burning up the miles in reverse order. I actually spun out on a few corners but I didn't care. There was lots of traffic now and I didn't feel conspicuous in the slightest.

Then, right in front of the Roost, at 8:30 on Sunday morning, in that snowstorm, I met the RCMP 4x4 coming the other way. I couldn't believe it. All lost after all.

I had the choice of turning down the Blueband turnoff and sneaking along the back route, but I remembered the voice of my biker friend Fingers Bailey from years ago: if you meet the cops the only thing to do is floor it for all you're worth, and in such matters I trusted bikers implicitly.

I broke over the hotel hill doing forty. I blasted through the snowbound Blueband turnoff doing sixty-five on the horizontal, a hundred on the up-and-down. I made the next turnoff in a ten-wheel drift. I broke over the little hump in front of the old man's with everything in the air. Lying in the back bedroom, he heard the crash I made landing and thought there'd been a vicious head-on collision outside. I went across the snow-slick Rowboat Pass bridge dead sideways. I took the mudhole in a final leap and sprang out the door in one motion, crescent wrench in hand, and began cranking out the licence plate bolts. I heard 4x4 tires turn off the pavement and start up the gravel. I scrambled up the clay bank and dove headlong into sticks, trees, wet salal brush, ripping a gash in my forehead. If they couldn't actually catch me at the wheel...

But it was just Ole and the boys coming to work in their 4x4. I walked out of the brush, grinning sheepishly, as they stared up in amazement. Then Ole saw the licence plate hanging by one bolt, the crescent wrench halfway up the bank, the fresh tire tracks, and doubled over laughing.

"He...thought...we...were...the COPS!" he gasped, turning red, and laughing, and laughing. As the other two put the clues together, they started laughing too. I chuckled reluctantly, with my mouth closed, standing stupidly at the top of the low clay bank, as they stomped and roared and pointed, then I opened my mouth and a few spontaneous laughs escaped, then before I knew what hit me I was lying at the bottom of the bank in wet clay howling my guts out as if I'd been born anew into the world. It took all three of them to unstick me from the clay, I laughed myself in so far.

"How did you ever end up with a job like that, anyway?" Egbert said as we mounted the last chipped concrete step and punched open the spring-loaded door of the Roost. He didn't seem at all affected by having watched me toil in the muck. He seemed bugged in some way.

Everyone in the pub looked up.

"Here he is. The garbage delight."

We picked a table by the window. Someone sent over a complimentary pitcher. I nodded in their general direction and told Egbert how I got the dump job.

"I take it you got back to your gravel pit and were able to satisfy the deputy whatever."

"Oh yeah. I worked until dark that Sunday and made it look like navvy jack heaven in there. The big shot walked up, took a handful of the pea-gravel and said 'There's nothing wrong with this material!' Reimer was screwed, though there was a lot of muttering about my 'going political' on them. I bumped into the Cedardale contractor in at Blueband Bluff Diesel shortly after and he was very huffy. But they had to give me the contract. The government big shot made sure of that, even wrote me after to see if everything was okay. It was him who designated me Supervisor of Solid Waste."

"So now you're the local hero." Egbert's tone was that of the stranger in town who suspects he's having one put over on him.

"No, but my wife can go to the post office, and Mrs. Quinlan confides she's afraid to take her garbage up unless I'm there to scare the bears, and when my little boy draws a stick-picture of me pushing a big bag of garbage with my cat, his teacher gives him a gold star and hangs it up for Parents Day. And no one asks me what I'm doing in that funny way any more."

"Yeah, but all this is nuts," he says.

"Maybe," I say. I really never have been sure.

JOKERVILLE

N.W. EMMOTT

HOUSING SHORTAGES have bedevilled Canadians, particularly young ones, for years. It was just as bad during the war years, when thousands of men were uprooted and sent to military stations. The men of the Royal Canadian Air Force prided themselves on the fact that they got all the good-looking girls. However, in those days it was taken for granted that you married the girl before you began to live with her, and that meant finding somewhere to live, since wives were not allowed in the barrack rooms.

When the war broke out, the Department of National Defence had strung air bases along the west coast of Vancouver Island, on the Queen Charlotte Islands, and along the fjord-indented coast between them. Some of them, like Ucluelet at the south end of Vancouver Island and Coal Harbour at the north end, Alliford Bay on the Queen Charlottes, and Bella Bella on the mainland, were all bases for seaplanes and flying boats. Later, runways were hacked out of the bush at places like Comox, Tofino and Port Hardy, and Sandspit in the Queen Charlotte Islands.

The stations were surprisingly big, and staffed exclusively with men. War is always fought largely by

boys, but a lot of the ground crew were older men who had plied dozens of trades in civvy street. Most of these mature men were married, and they missed their families. Furthermore, the young regulars seemed to have as the foremost idea in their heads that they wanted to get married too. And here they were, perched on the rim of the world with nothing to do but their duty and nowhere to go but a movie once a week in the drill hall.

There were no nearby villages to bring their wives to. If the men wanted their wives with them, they would have to build houses for themselves. They set to work.

The houses were not elaborate—mere cabins, without such modern cossetings as running water, electric power or indoor plumbing. The war would not go on forever, and after the last shots were fired the air stations would go back to the bush. Furthermore, airmen were frequently transferred. What the situation called for was a cabin, not a house, that could be abandoned without a qualm.

With surprising speed, tiny towns sprang up near the air stations. A location near one of the roads leading to the base, reasonably open, would be chosen and cleared. Lots would be picked out. There were always men who had built houses before, and would know how much lumber to order, and how much hardware. Arrangements would be made to buy the lumber at a mill, which would be fifty or sixty miles away, and to transport it on a barge or a fishing boat. Prices were reasonable: in 1940 at Ucluelet, first-grade lumber could be bought for $20 a thousand board feet. A couple of decades later, two boards would cost that much.

The men would then hurry out to their selected sites and set to work building their cabins as soon as they finished supper every night. Most of them were handy with tools, and airmen who were skilled carpenters would advise them. The cabins came out summer-cottage style, with perhaps two rooms: a bedroom and another room for everything else. At the rear there would be an outhouse, and water could be carried from a convenient spring (in the west coast rainforest, there was always a spring available). There would be a woodstove to provide heat and to cook on, sometimes aided by a Coleman kerosene stove, and kerosene or gasoline lamps for lighting. The beds were generally built-in, with bedsprings and mattresses resting on wooden frames. Sometimes the springs were omitted, and the mattresses rested on the boards. Tables and chairs were often homemade, and bathtubs were generally old-fashioned round galvanized iron tubs hung on a nail at the back of the house when not in use.

Three hundred dollars could build a cabin in those palmy days. Of course, a month's wages for a Leading Aircraftsman with marriage allowance would only be about $120 a month. When he was transferred, the owner could sell it to his successor. The land cost nothing, since the people were actually squatters on Crown land. Out in the bush, nobody bothered with building permits or titles.

Conditions seemed primitive, but the people were young and strong, and not many of them had been used to luxury. Born in the Depression, they considered that a steady job and money to spend made up for a great deal. Besides, the average length of stay at a bush station was only a year or so. The climate was mild enough to make spartan living conditions bearable; indeed, it was like living in a summer cottage.

The young wives were quite happy with their lot. The community was close-knit, with somebody nearby to help if emergencies arose. The facilities of an air base — the snack bar, the recreation hall, the gymnasium, the hospital and the various messes at certain times — were open to them, even if on a sub-rosa basis. The air stations installed washing machines for the use of the men, which the women could use, and they were welcome to watch the movies and attend the shows put on by touring entertainment groups. Best of all, the wives were able to go to the air base to take showers. A good many children were born, and as long as they were pre-school age, there was no problem.

Jack Munn and Lawrence Foan fitting a frame for the front door.

As time went on, the instant married quarters became organized. The men got together and built sidewalks, while sometimes Air Force bulldozers and graders would mysteriously appear and scratch out roads. A "mayor" would be elected, and a "town council." The residents all took turns, according to a roster compiled by the mayor, in doing jobs like collecting garbage and keeping sidewalks in repair.

The Commanding Officer of the air base either turned a blind eye to the villages or encouraged them. A married man living with his wife got into no trouble in the wet canteen, nor did he gamble in the barracks, and he did not get into brawls over women at fish canneries and Indian reserves. Besides, the married men were always the most skilled and reliable tradesmen.

I lived in one of these villages twice. In 1940, I was stationed at Ucluelet while it was still being hacked out of the bush. Still single at the time, I had no interest in setting up housekeeping, but I did lend a hand to one of my friends who was building a cabin for his new wife. Then in 1945 I was posted to Port Hardy.

Port Hardy had a well-established married patch, which rejoiced in the name of "Jokerville." Originally built by airmen, it had been expanded by employees of Pan American Airways, who serviced a staging point for aircraft flying a shuttle service between Seattle and Alaska. These Americans thought big; they piped in running water and installed an electric generator. Unfortunately, by the time I got there, Pan American had put larger aircraft into service and eliminated the staging stop. They pulled out their men and their diesel generator as well. The lights went out, but the water kept coming. The "mayor" organized a roster to patrol the pipe leading to the spring which supplied the water, to make sure there were no leaks or breaks caused by trees falling across it. There was no distinction of rank in selecting people to man the patrol.

One of the cabins in Jokerville was available, since its occupant had just been transferred away. I bought it for $300. It was a two-room affair with a wooden platform eighteen inches high jutting out into the building from one wall. A partition divided it in two; the side jutting into the kitchen became a couch, while the other side became the bed.

The house had one great luxury—there was a water-heating coil in the woodstove, which fed a shower installed in a little tin-sided stall built into a corner of the kitchen. The stove had another benefit: we could dry the washing in the kitchen, since it was generally foggy and clothes took days to dry in the open. There was also a sink in the kitchen, a luxury by no means to be discounted.

After I had bought the cabin, I wrote to my wife, who was staying in Vancouver, asking her to come up to Port Hardy and to bring along a mattress and some bedding. She brought it up in a single-engine Norseman floatplane, which landed at the nearby Indian village, Fort Rupert. An Indian boy in a rowboat saw the plane taxiing back and forth uncertainly in the harbour, and brought her to shore, where I was waiting for her in a jeep. I took her proudly back to her new house, and if she was dismayed, she hid it very well. Actually, it compared favourably with the gardener's cottage in which we had begun our married life in Sidney, before I went overseas.

Setting up housekeeping was easy. Our predecessors had left their furniture (a kitchen table and two chairs) and a few cooking utensils. We put our mattress on the wooden bed, without benefit of a spring, and covered it with the sheets my wife had brought and blankets and pillows I had borrowed from the air station.

An axe went with the cabin, and the surrounding forest was full of firewood. I noticed, however, that I seemed to be the only person doing much chopping. One of my neighbours enlightened me.

"Just get some coal from George," he counselled.

The air base furnaces burned coal, which was freighted in from Nanaimo on a barge. The barge was moored at a pier at the end of the road that went through Jokerville. Residents helped themselves to

Cabin built at Ucluelet by Sgt. Lawrence Foan (right), 1940. That same year, Margery Foan (left) gave birth to the first child born in Ucluelet in twenty-seven years.

Cabins at Alliford Bay, 1943.

T. Benson's cabin, Alliford Bay, 1943.

enough fuel for their stoves, and the RCAF never missed it. Neither did King George, who strictly speaking owned it.

With ample supplies of coal, my wife soon became the social leader of the community. Our house was the only one with hot water and a shower, and the other ladies would gather each morning, bringing goodies and taking turns having showers, while the rest drank coffee and discussed the state of the world. After the coffee-and-shower visit was over, however, social leadership reverted to the wife of a sergeant, in her forties, who had lived on a Saskatchewan farm on the edge of civilization and knew exactly how to do everything required in a frontier environment.

Like all self-respecting villages, Jokerville had its dogs and cats. The commanding officer of the station, who had brought his wife to Jokerville, found out all about them one day when he, a pious fisherman, had caught a salmon whose magnificence astounded all who saw it. He brought it proudly back to his cabin and hung it on a nail while he went inside to get his camera. He was briefly delayed inside the house, and when he reappeared with his camera he found nothing left of the fish except the skeleton, while a number of neighbours' cats sat about, cleaning their whiskers. Cats take orders from nobody, not even the commanding officer.

The wives bought their supplies at a store on the Kwakiutl Indian Reserve at Fort Rupert about three miles away. A coastal steamer would call there every ten days, bringing meat and vegetables and other groceries. When the women heard the boat's whistle they would walk over and wait on the steps of the store, while the manager drove to the wharf in his dilapidated truck to pick up the cargo consigned to him. He was a very capable young man of about nineteen, the son of the store's owner, who never seemed to be around. The women would inspect the goods—it was strictly self-service there—and take what they needed to make up their orders. The young man would cut up the meat, which generally came as quarters, and sell it for three prices, as stew meat, steaks or roasts. He was not too familiar with the various cuts, however, and on one occasion he sold a tenderloin to my wife, charging it as stewing beef. At the prices he charged, however, he was in no danger of bankruptcy.

The store had that wonderful general-store smell of oil and coffee and soap and leather. Some of the goods on the shelves had been there for some time, the proprietor being confident everything would sell eventually. Wandering about one day, I saw a can of Postum, which I liked, and I bought it. When I got it home, however, I found that it was frozen as hard as iron, having been on the shelf for probably twenty years. I had to use a hammer and chisel to get enough out of the can to make myself a cup. City slickers who liked Postum were not too common in Fort Rupert.

Life in Jokerville was pleasant if you could stand the social life. Somebody had a party every night, and everybody around would come. Then one night when we had decided to stay home, a jeep pulled up in front of our cabin and several of the single men with whom I worked at the base piled out. Bored with their humdrum life at the base, they had decided to sample the delights of Jokerville. They brought with them coffee and some butter, which was rationed in those days. We spent the evening playing word games and drinking tea and coffee, and had a marvellous time. This happened frequently after that, and everyone always had a good time.

One day several of us sailed aboard a fishing boat, helping to pull our salmon in. When we docked we took a couple of salmon back to our cabin, where one of the group informed us that he knew exactly how to fillet and fry fish. He lived up to his boast. One of the men with us, who came from Ontario, told us that he had never tasted fish and never would. After he tasted one of the fillets he ate twice as many of them as anybody else.

There was not much news in Jokerville. There was no electricity to drive ordinary radios, although the men could listen to the radio at the air station and report to their wives on what they had heard. I had a battery-powered radio, however, which I had wired up to hot-shot batteries when the irreplaceable batteries that had come with the set expired, and the women listened in on that during their kaffee klatsches at our cabin. Thus it was that when I came home one evening my wife told me excitedly that President Truman had reported that a bomb as powerful as 20,000 tons of TNT had been dropped on Japan. With my superior knowledge I assured her that she must have been mistaken—it could only have been 20,000 pounds. I had to climb down later when I found out she had been right.

With the war over, the little cabins in the bush were deserted when the air stations were closed down and the families went back home. Forty years later, my wife and I visited Port Hardy again and tried to find the first house we had ever owned. It had completely disappeared. Our memories of it, however, remain.

WADDINGTON
—AND THE—
CHILCOTIN
WAR

SCOTTY MCINTYRE

AMONG THE FIRST WAVE of gold-seekers to arrive in Victoria in 1858 was an Englishman named Alfred Waddington, who on arrival set himself up as a merchant in the settlement and immediately displayed an active interest in the political and commercial affairs of the island and the mainland.

In November 1858, he published the first book printed in the two colonies, entitled *The Fraser Mines Vindicated, or The History of Four Months* and printed by P. de Garro, printer, Wharf Street, Victoria. In this volume is an impartial description of Victoria at that time: "there were 800 inhabitants, there was no noise, bustle, gamblers, speculators or parties with special interests to preach up this or that—only gentlemanly inhabitants, mostly Scotchmen, there was no business and the streets were overgrown with grass and there was not even a cart. Flour was scarce and at times there was no bread for several days."

Such was Victoria when two men named McDonald and Adams walked into Spokane with a bag of gold they had taken from the bars of the Fraser and Thompson rivers. The rush was on.

At first the miners were inclined to get to the diggings via Puget Sound, thus avoiding British territory and American miners. Speculators were quick to fan the flames of patriotism, and streets were laid out and lots sold at Whatcom. As an added incentive, the miners were advised that the Bellingham Bay trail would

VOL. 3.   VICTORIA, VANCOUVER ISLAND, SATURDAY, AUGUST 13, 1859.   NO. 8.

VIEW OF FORT YALE, FRASER RIVER.

be cut, which would form a clear path to the Fraser and Thompson rivers. This statement was made without any idea of the swamps, mountains and rough terrain this trail would have to cross.

After waiting several weeks for the trail to open, the hordes of miners who had gathered at Whatcom began to realize that it was only a speculator's dream, and it being proved that the Fraser was navigable by paddlewheelers as far as Fort Yale, they headed for Victoria in large numbers, swamping the settlement and sending the prices of supplies skyrocketing (the Hudson's Bay Company and the four or five other stores in the area could charge whatever they pleased). This ended the peace of Victoria. Then Governor James Douglas decided to build a wagon road from Yale to the Cariboo. Alfred Waddington, a promoter, immediately took issue with the scheme, pointing out that the logical place for a road was from the head of Bute Inlet, up the Homathko River valley to the Chilcotin. To prove his point, he gave the following statistics:

	Bute Inlet	Yale–Fraser Canyon Route
Ship navigation	305 miles	182 miles
Land travel	185 miles	359 miles
Days consumed packing freight	22	37

In spite of these figures, Douglas insisted on the Canyon route, so in 1861, Waddington formed a company to build the Bute Inlet Wagon Road and applied for a charter that would enable that company to collect tolls on all goods crossing the route. This charter was granted in 1862, and the route was mapped out. It was decided to follow the Homathko River valley, cross Mount Waddington at an elevation of 2,000 feet, with steep grades until it reached the plateau, and then swing northeast, connecting with the Bentinck Arm Trail at Puntzi Lake.

By April 1864, a pack trail had been cut for about forty miles up the valley and a crew of sixteen men under foreman William Brewster, with sixteen Indian packers, were employed on the project. A ferry had been rigged up to cross the Homathko and placed under the charge of Timothy Smith.

On April 7, a Chilcotin Indian named Klatassine came to visit his son, who was one of the packers, and he was accompanied by a chief named Tallot. There was a conference between those men and the packers, and from then on, according to one of the white men, the packers were surly, unco-operative and rebellious.

On April 29, Klatassine, Tallot and another Indian arrived at the ferry and demanded food from Smith. This request was refused, and Smith was shot down and his body flung into the river. The food stores were then looted and half a ton of provisions were seized and cached nearby. The Indians, now reinforced, advanced to the construction camp at a place now known as Murderers Bar, where they camped down at the packers' camp. That night, suspecting nothing, all the men retired, three to a tent, some hundred yards from the Indian camp.

At daylight on April 30, the Indians struck. The tent cords were cut, collapsing the poles, and as the men struggled to disentangle themselves from their canvas covering, they were struck with knives and axes. Three of them did manage to get out. Peterson Dane, though struck with an axe and shot through the arm, plunged into the river and was swept down to a bar where he managed to crawl ashore. A man named Buckley, who had been stabbed and left for dead, managed to crawl into the bush hours later. Edwin Mosley managed to get out and hide in the bush, and he was somehow unhurt although his two tent-mates had been killed. Those three survivors met and made their way to the ferry, only to find that it had been cut adrift and swept down the river. Buckley, who had been a sailor, rigged up a travelling loop on the ferry cable that was still in place. By this means, the three men crossed the river and made their way to the head of Bute Inlet, where they procured a canoe and managed to return to civilization to spread the news of the massacre.

Meanwhile, back at Murderers Bar, the Indians disposed of their victims' bodies by flinging them into the river. Some four miles upstream, they came upon Brewster and three men who were blazing a trail, and killed them before the men could resist. Brewster's body was mutilated and left lying where it fell; the other three were tossed into the river. The assassins, now numbering thirty, advanced into the Chilcotin, where they claimed another victim: William Manning, a settler, who was shot on his homestead at Puntzi Lake. Klatassine then received word that a pack train was coming along the Bentinck Trail and immediately made arrangements to attack. The train, loaded with supplies for the Bute Inlet Road, had eight drivers under the command of Alexander McDonald, an experienced driver who knew the country well. An Indian woman warned McDonald of the impending attack, but he ignored her and ordered the train to proceed—right into the ambush. The Indians, now numbering fifty or sixty, fired from behind the trees lining the trail and killed three drivers in the ensuing battle.

Fear spread among the white population throughout the interior, and many settlers and miners left for the coast.

News of the massacre of the road builders reached New Westminster on May 14, and Governor Frederick Seymour, within a month of arriving to become Governor of the colony, found himself face to face with what appeared to be a genuine Indian war. However, he took steps to face up to the situation immediately. The next day, twenty-eight volunteers under the command of Chartres Brew, head of the British Columbia constabulary, were dispatched by the HMS *Forward* to the Chilcotin via Bute Inlet.

Another party of fifty volunteers was formed at Quesnellemouth, under William Cox, a gold commissioner. Among them were Donald McLean, formerly a chief trader for the Hudson's Bay Company at Kamloops, and his two sons. This party was to go overland and rendezvous with the Brew party at Puntzi Lake. Cox's party was delayed while the *Enterprise* underwent repairs, but arrived in Puntzi Lake on June 12. They sent out a scouting party, which promptly fell into an ambush. Cox decided to build a fort and await reinforcements.

Meanwhile, the Brew party had made its way to the end of the trail on the Homathko, and finding no way to get through to the Chilcotin, they had abandoned the attempt and returned to New Westminster. There, another party of thirty-eight volunteers quickly formed. Under Brew's command and accompanied by Governor Seymour, they boarded the HMS *Sutlej* with the intention of reaching the Chilcotin via the Bentinck Arm trail. After landing at the head of the arm, they met the five survivors of the McDonald party and learned of the new massacre. Fears of a full-scale war grew, though the men were calmed somewhat when they found the Bella Coola Indians quite friendly and willing to do everything in their power to assist the expedition. Proceeding slowly inland, the Brew party soon came upon the scene of the struggle between the Indians and McDonald's men. Kegs of nails, tools and looted packsacks were strewn in all directions, and a deserted Indian blockhouse with loopholed walls had been destroyed. Of Indians, however, there was no sign.

They reached Puntzi Lake and met Cox on July 7. Ten days later, Donald McLean went out with an Indian guide to reconnoiter, and when the guide heard the click of a gun, he lay down and advised McLean to do the same. McLean refused and was shot through the heart. The guide made his way back to camp, and a party was sent out to retrieve the body. Brew's party now set off to search the country toward the coast, while Cox's party stayed in camp.

Alexis, a Chilcotin chief, was finally persuaded to present himself to the Governor. With him was a slave sent by Klatassine to ask for the terms of their surrender. Cox packed the slave with a sack of flour and other articles, gave assurances of friendship and invited them into the camp, which had now been moved to the old Hudson's Bay Company fort on the Chusko River. The next day, Klatassine, Tallot and six others arrived at the fort, accompanied by Chief Alexis and some of his people. They gave a horse, a mule, money and gold dust to the Governor as tokens of good faith. Then they informed him that of the thirteen others involved in the murders, ten could not be reached until the following spring, one had been shot by McDonald and the other two had committed suicide.

The Indians were surprised and bitter when they suddenly found themselves surrounded by armed men, had their weapons taken from them and were bound as prisoners. The *British Columbian* of September 17

Governor James Douglas.

stated that "Cox made representation of friendship and immunity which he could not perform," and at the trial, Judge Matthew Baillie Begbie noted that "those men were induced to surrender." Although Cox denied the accusations, it seems they must have been accurate. What other reason could there be for the surrender of men whom the whites had not been able to find a trace of, and who could easily have holed up in the Cascades indefinitely?

Now that the ringleaders were secured, Cox's party returned to Alexandria with the prisoners and Brew's party went on to Bella Coola.

What caused the outbreak? There seems no doubt that while the road builders were well supplied with food, the Indian packers were nearly starved. Food was the only thing they took, both at the ferry and at the camp. Tools, money and personal effects were found where the workers had left them.

Begbie stated at the trial that the interference with Indian lands, especially with some valuable spring water, was one of the roots of the trouble, and the *British Columbian* stated "the treatment received by the packers at the hands of Brewster and his party was at once calculated to arouse their cupidity and provoke their vengeance." Another complaint of the Indians was the desecration of their graves by the white men; this grievance was later taken seriously to the point that in 1865, the attorney general introduced an ordinance to the Legislative Council that made this offence punishable by a fine of £100 and six months' imprisonment.

The trial of the defendants took place in Quesnellemouth before Judge Begbie in September 1864. Of the eight defendants, two became Crown witnesses, five were found guilty and hanged and the other was sentenced to life imprisonment, but he escaped custody. The expedition into the Chilcotin had cost the colony about $80,000, and an application to the Imperial Government to bear half of this cost was turned down by the Secretary of State. The widow of Donald McLean was granted an annuity of £100 per year for five years. Waddington then petitioned the government for compensation amounting to $50,000 on the grounds that the government had given his party no protection. The Legislative Council turned him down: no protection had been requested, there had been no notification that the road builders were in that area, and no state could guarantee its citizens safe from murder.

Although the incident had destroyed the Bute Inlet road scheme, Waddington was still convinced that the route was feasible. As late as 1867, he was still trying to get his charter renewed. By this time he was also deeply involved in a scheme for building a coast-to-coast railway in British North America, a project with which he was so obsessed that people began to think of him as a visionary and a bit of a bore. In 1868, he went to London at his own expense to lay before the House of Commons a petition for a railway via the Yellowhead Pass Bute Inlet route. He was listened to with polite interest only, but when he got back to Ottawa, he learned that his scheme was already assured by the Terms of Union, a Canada-U.S. treaty. The government purchased his plans as being a great help to the surveyors and engineers who would be engaged to push the road through.

Unfortunately, Waddington never lived to see his dream come true: he died of smallpox in Ottawa in 1871.

The Only Jews in Gibsons Landing

DAN PROPP

IN 1950 when I was five years old we moved from Sucre, Bolivia to Gibsons Landing. We were the only Jews in Gibsons Landing. Were we German, Jewish, Bolivian, Canadian? What were we doing here? We weren't even "here" except in the physical sense. We were still in flight from the yellow star, the death, still escaping. There were endless walks to the post office for letters from Germany, Bolivia, Brazil, England and Israel. There were the stories, the love of German, the hate of German, a little Goethe, a little Yiddish thrown together in a constant torrent that could only be kept bearable for a five-year-old by the saving grace of the water, the islands, the government wharf, the fresh air, the fishing!

Down by Armour's Float one could gaze down into that magic blue-green water and see the shiners that loved the seaworms, or the perch that preferred the little crabs carefully lifted from under specific types of rocks that only those of us in the know knew about.

We always knew a city slicker by the kind of worm he selected. They didn't have the nerve to obtain the good ones, the special thick type that practically kissed the end of shiner hooks. The kids from Vancouver just used puny garden worms that turned to liquid when you touched them! But our sea worms slipped with pride.

During our first few years down on the Gibsons Landing waterfront, long before Bruno Gerussi and the Beachcombers, the old passenger ship *The Mashigone* (a converted fishpacker) and Union steamships sailed past our rented waterfront home. They looked like jewels between Keats Island and the concrete steps from our front lawn. We could sit on the steps at high tide, dangle our feet in the water and imagine ourselves in paradise. The bell from the camp on Keats rang, seaweed massaged our toes, a seagull we named Emma sat on a piling, and the sound of older children diving off the deep end of Armour's Float made the scene complete, like a modern West Coat Camelot.

One day a new vessel glided past, carrying automobiles as well as passengers. Rather a beautiful sight, in the twilight of a spectacular sunset. We nevertheless sensed the kind of change that wildlife and children feel, react to but can't express. There was a stirring in the air, subtle but unquestionably there.

No longer did the majesty of the Union Steamships' *Lady Cecelia*, complete with white tablecloths and fine dining room, grace our village. The converted fish-packer that had delivered us from Horseshoe Bay to this never-never land also vanished. Gone was the black stove in the hold where a Norwegian named Ole made buttered toast and fried eggs such as I have never tasted since. Along the Black Ball Line's *Smokwa* came cafeteria-style dining and fast food.

However, we were still safe from television and plastic cups. Eisenhower was still playing golf and our local motion picture theatre broadened our horizons as well as it could with the Movietone News.

Sometimes an amphibious human-made dragonfly dropped out of the sky and peacefully floated in to tie up at Armour's Float. The hatch would open and two or three bemused faces look out as a group of kids—myself included—hung their mouths open in wonder. This was modern innovation at its best. Seaplanes in themselves were a wonder but the insect-like amphibious type demanded disbelief.

One morning we were playing on an old twisted log in front of the sand bank where the choice seaworms lived. For the present the bait was safe from the scavenging children because the tide was almost in. A small strip of water-free beach remained. Two of us fell off the log. The other kids hit the beach first and I tumbled on top. Neither of us was any worse for wear, but as I stood up, the boy's father yelled to his son, "Go punch that dirty Jew!"

At the appropriate time, my father instructed me to send that child a birthday card. It read "Happy Birthday, from the dirty Jew."

Handlines were not a major problem, but acquiring the prestige that came with using a proper rod and reel became my nemesis. The name of the game was to use a heavy sinker with a live shiner on a big hook and cast like a trooper. The further the line went, the better it felt. Sometimes an unsophisticated seagull (probably from the city) jumped in for the shiner. The spectacle then became similar to flying a kite. The line went up! Invariably the bird skillfully separated the fish from the hook or simply let go. A breath of relief quickly followed because we were all deathly worried about being fined sixty dollars for killing a seagull.

Tangled lines were a constant problem, especially when there was seaweed in the water. The other children seemed to have a knack for undoing the knots. I didn't — I relied upon scissors. My lines shrank daily. Eventually my mother came to the rescue. If her child came running home with a beautiful rock cod, complete with monstrous head and bulging eyes, guess who cut off its head with a saw and then did the cleaning? Not I, oh no. My job was the catching and possibly the eating, if there were not too many bones.

One day a friend of my dad's, one who didn't have much of an affinity for children, reluctantly agreed to take me salmon fishing out in the gap. At the first sign of dawn, when the moon was almost gone, I met him at the base of the float. He looked at the rod, uncut herring strip, flashers and Tom Mack spoon I'd brought along. The old man simply shook his head, said nothing, inhaled a deep breath of the crisp pre-dawn air and proceeded silently to the boat. I followed, in deference, a few feet behind, looking toward the gap and the tops of the trees, hoping they weren't moving. Possibly, just possibly the water past Gospel Rock, Salmon Rock and Gower Point would be calm, like glass.

When I saw the tops of the trees moving it was time to rationalize that the wind really didn't exist and . . . if perhaps a little breeze was blowing it would remain at tree level but not reach the water's surface. The thought of waves gave me a cold sweat. Seasickness was terror even to contemplate.

I gingerly put one foot in the sixteen-foot rowboat with a built-in "putt-putt" engine. The second foot reluctantly followed suit. I hid under the cloth-covered bow and worried.

Two or three skillful tugs on the rope and the old Briggs and Stratton lawn mower-type engine sprang into action. Now there was nothing more that I could do but hope, smell the oil-gas mixture and think of the *wrrrr* of the reel, the proper playing of the salmon, the ultimate weakening of its resistance, the anticipation of pulling it in and hoping the net yielded a salmon, not a dogfish.

Gibsons Landing quickly shrank, the buoy grew in size and the ripples enlarged too. The then-undeveloped bluff we used to climb came into view. The ripples began rocking and then rolling. The smell of the oil-gas mixture intensified.

We trolled from Salmon Rock to Gospel Rock and my white face turned to green. I got not so much as a nibble, the old man caught his limit, and my condition ended with the anticipated conclusion. From that time on I was banished. I was allowed to fish only from the Government Wharf or Armour's Float.

Perhaps the waves had represented the actual turbulence, the flight, the realization that one's very being was a product of Dad's inner soul, twisted like the feared knock of the Gestapo in the middle of the night. The knock was a sound my father and mother might

33

actually have heard. I only hear about the knock, constantly, from their stories. We who as children listened, now in later years are haunted by their stories that in youth we attempted.

I knew that I was a "dirty Jew" in the eyes of someone who didn't even know me, had never even spoken to me. I knew that in the fresh air, and in the early morning mists of the islands, I was one, I was whole, complete, together, accepted.

While Dad operated a small rented sawmill, cutting lumber to be sent directly to Bolivia for the tin mines, I went to school, a mile away from the mill. The school was surrounded by magnificent maple trees and a concrete foundation ideal for playing marbles against. I would look through the cat's-eyes, crystals and cobs that we played with at recess and lunch, and in the refracted light I would dream of holidays and fishing. In the motion of the Maypole and the flutter of the Union Jack one felt at home. . .almost.

Dad always said that we were like short stubby trees. We survived the winds, our roots were strong but our shapes became somewhat bent over because of the difficulties. Feeling completely at home was something we could ill afford. Indeed, it was a dangerous and false feeling, in light of what had occurred in Germany.

Dad didn't want to inflict the family tradition of the lumber industry upon his son. His solution was that I should become a dentist. The financial rewards may indeed have had some merit, but the prospect of open mouths, saliva and worried looks didn't sit well with me. For a child with a history of toothaches, decay, slow drills and extrications, even teacher seemed like saint, compared to dentists.

On my twelfth birthday my parents gave me a present with which I came closest to achieving or creating a sense, a purpose, a youthful foundation. It was a twenty-four-dollar Kodak developing kit. Photography became a passion that I carried with me into adulthood. My peers went through normal puberty; I went through developers, fixers and tons of enlarging paper. My parents went through the wall, experiencing a bathroom turned darkroom with chemical stains everywhere.

My parents were most patient in this regard. Their enthusiasm for my photographic "fishing" had to do with its more practical ramifications. Besides, it was safer. At least there were fewer worries about their son being on the water.

Dad, however, didn't have much success understanding our changing society. To consider a wringer washer was an insult. The little cooler outside our kitchen window sufficed for a refrigerator, even during the summer. The antique oil stove with the regu-larly plugged-up pipe was always available. So, what was one to worry?

Dad's stoicism must have originated in his childhood. His father, also in the sawmill business, had gone broke, and declaring bankruptcy in Germany, especially during that era, meant shame for the entire family. Here in Canada it had almost become a national pastime, certainly in Gibsons Landing. Bankruptcy was declared one day, a new enterprise attempted the next and, well, there was always welfare. Dad could not conceive of this kind of life. To have enough food on the table, independence and health meant everything. Nothing else was of consequence. Squandering of any kind was frowned upon—a principle that manifested itself so profoundly on one of his birthdays that both my mother and I had to head for the hills until his mood improved.

I had somehow saved up six dollars to purchase a bottle of imported French champagne. My mother actually did the honours, because minors couldn't even enter a liquor store in those days. When I lovingly presented my father with the bottle he paused for a moment, attempted to restrain his true feelings and then, like a volcano, totally exploded. He fumed at both of us for having even considered such waste.

The "hills" we ran to was an apartment upstairs, where a pleasant young couple lived. As we were led in and offered coffee and 7-Up, a loud slam and angry departing footsteps vibrated downstairs. Dad was on the warpath. Tears streamed down my face as I studied the bottle of cool green pop that read, "You like it. It likes you." Mom was trying to be cordial. Our hosts were trying to pretend that all was well. Osgoode Conklin was bellowing at Eve Arden. Our Miss Brooks held us in her entertaining grasp.

Like the waves and tides, the calmness of peace returned an hour or so later, the downstairs door gently closed and we knew that it was safe to return.

We were not practising Jews in the traditional sense. I knew nothing of keeping the Sabbath, kosher meals, separate dishes, Passover, Yom Kippur or any of the traditions common to most Jewish children. Yet deep inside I had a longing for something somehow familiar, yet never really experienced. With fishing line or camera, in a sense I was always fishing or framing a purpose, perhaps even an understanding that "normal" children don't experience.

The memories of my parents will always live. Their stories of escape, adjustment in Bolivia and again in Canada reverberate in the mists of the shore, in the movement of the tide. And like fishermen in middle age, we attempt to untangle the lines. In a sense, we children of the survivors will always be children, trying to untangle the lines.

GHOSTWOOD

JOHN LIVINGSTONE

This valley is companied by ghosts.
Stumps, bramblegrown, evidence old forest
felled many years gone.
Clawed rays depict, even through new growth,
where the towers sat.
Little imagining hears howling, heavy diesels,
whistle, cries of men
that saturate sidehills stoled in mist.
The blurred silhouette of gilpoked
deadfall and root
recalls the prehistoric head of a grapple-loader
ever hungry for new-found logs.

But it is people I remember,
people who claimed,
in this strange mix of boredom and death
a way to live, a place to be.
They were men who found for a little while
pride in an excellence
others would shun from fear
or simple inability.
It was frenchy, wooden tit, the prince of denmark,
the duck, twinkletoes, plumjam, the bear
and so many more,
nicknames evoking memories
completed in their blood.

Most of them are now real ghosts,
victims of the widow maker,
caught in the snap of a siwash
jumping from a stump,
murdered by hangups,
or in an explosion of rotten hemlock
a hundred years conked.
There are so many, many ways to die.

But life was real,
framed in the sharp tang of cypress,
hemlock dyed hands, jaggered chokers,
blackflies in summer dawn,
hoar frost rime in winter,
smoked sweat fear smell
from hungry fire running free
through standing timber.

And I remember my part,
for I, too, lived this life now gone.
I remember the gasping breath
fighting more than a hundredweight block and strap
a thousand feet up sidehill six foot snow covered
through the jumble of two hundred foot pick-up
  sticks.

I remember the clear winter mornings
pungent in woods scents,
embellished in the distant sound
of a mountain borne wolf pack,
or watching the otters' snaky dance and slide across
    ice.

I remember the oscillating growl of a sixty-six-foot
    boomstick
searching for some titanic baseball
as I ducked in reflex,
too late, but thankful to have heard.

I remember the endless repetition
and stale tobacco foul mouthed men.

I remember the pride of these people
who lived and postured
in the knowledge that what they did
could not be written in a text
for any idle person to eye and mouthe.

It has vanished.
Bunkhouses gone, camps deserted,
the very work is now in disrepute,
not through the loggers' fault,
though they, each one,
bear brunt of public censure
companies ignore
in their profits' grasp.

The phantoms left
rot in the scorched duff
of slashed hills,
mute testimony to the greed
that prostitutes person and resource alike,
a gold rush
whose butter glint lies in corporate fingering
of new felled wood,
whose fever consumes lives
burning nutrient from trunk and limb
and leaches from the land
soils' fertility to bear again,
slaying God's garden's growth.

the FABLE of the FLOOD

RICHARD ATLEO

SON OF CRANE decided it was time to marry. So he went to see Miss Sawbill. No one could blame Crane for his decision, because, as everyone knows, Miss Sawbill is really quite pretty.

When Crane arrived he came right to the point and with great ceremony announced, "I'm going to marry you."

"No!" Miss Sawbill remonstrated, "I can't. You're not good enough. Besides, you're too ugly."

Crane was taken aback. Not good enough? Too ugly? True, he was not the handsomest fellow in the world, but everyone knows that looks aren't everything. Ugly indeed! Miss Sawbill would be sorry she insulted him. With revenge in his heart Crane went to see Wren for some advice.

"What shall I do?" Crane asked. "Miss Sawbill doesn't want to marry me. She says that I'm not good enough, that I'm too ugly."

Wren could see that Crane sought revenge so he thought for a moment. Then he said, "Nothing to it. Go to the mountain. Go right to the top and look for a large yellow cedar tree. Climb this tree and stand facing the south. Stretch out your arms in supplication and chant this song four times:

> Nana wa nin sin ke ee
> Cloo putch ma kin see ke ee
> She said to me . . . She said to me . . .
> Let the seas rise, let the tides come in.

When you have done that you will see the seas rise and flood the land."

So Crane went up the mountain. He found a large yellow cedar tree and climbed it. He faced toward the south and with arms outstretched he began to chant:

> Nana wa nin sin ke ee
> Cloo putch ma kin see ke ee
> She said to me . . . She said to me . . .
> Let the seas rise, let the tides come in.

Four times he chanted the song and when he had finished he saw something far to the south. He saw the

seas begin to rise. Slowly at first and then faster and faster. Soon he saw the tides raging everywhere, flooding all the land. The tides splashed and swirled up the great mountainsides. The tides rose until water covered everything except the mountaintop where Crane stood. For a long time the water covered the land, covered all access to food. All the land birds drowned while all the sea birds had great difficulty in finding food.

When the flood had receded, Crane saw that his revenge had been too great. He saw the Robin, the Wren, the Eagle, and all the other land birds dead. Swiftly Crane restored them all to life so that none of them knew that they had been dead.

Meanwhile Miss Sawbill had been carried far to the south by the raging tide. Because of her refusal to marry Crane she was destined to travel south each year all by herself. Each year she must return from the south all by herself. When she mates she must bear her young and raise them without the help of Mr. Sawbill. Even today you can see Miss Sawbill travelling and raising her young all by herself.

the HISTORIC FLOOD

RICHARD ATLEO

PEOPLE ALL OVER THE WORLD have stories about the flood. The Bible says that Noah was warned about a coming flood and accordingly told what to do. This account of a flood comes from an old man who lives in Ahousat, British Columbia.

This story is not a fable, but a historical account of the flood as it was passed down to us. People in those days lived far and wide as they do today. Some lived where there were no mountains and others like ourselves lived by the mountains.

Gnahss (God) warned the people that He would flood the world. "Be prepared. Clothe yourselves for I will flood the world. There will be no food and neither will you have any means of getting food."

No one knew how long the flood would last. One man amongst many was instructed in how best he could survive. "Take your large canoe and stock it with hardy roots and herbs that do not rot easily. Fashion a long rope and anchor it to a Tse-weep plant at the base of Lone Cone Mountain."

The man took heed and did as he was instructed. He gathered the roots and herbs that could be eaten raw; he fashioned a long rope and anchored it to the Tse-weep plant, which resists rot under water. The plant has the further advantage of having deep roots which are difficult to pull out.

When he was ready the tide began to rise. The tide swirled and raged in every direction. As the tide rose

there were those who climbed the mountains to escape. When they could go no higher the waters surged over them and swept their bodies away. Others who had gotten into their canoes but did not anchor them drifted at the mercy of the racing water.

Up and up the waters rose until nothing could be seen except the swiftly raging waters. Many perished.

It is not known for how long the flood lasted but only those who had prepared survived it. Those who had followed the instructions to anchor on the Tse-weep found themselves on their own land when the floods receded. So it was that the man who had anchored at the base of Lone Cone Mountain landed on top of it. When the tides became normal again he descended the mountain with his family.

Those who had not anchored their canoes drifted far. It is said that people drifted as far as Neah Bay, Washington. Wherever they landed the local tribes took them in and some became slaves. It is said too that this mixing of people is the reason that the old people understand other tribal languages. After the first flood the various languages changed somewhat because strangers brought new words. Words which the local tribes accepted into their languages. For example a group from Ahousat may have landed at Pachina while a group from another tribe may have landed at Ahousat. Each group would influence the other's language.

Today, it is said, there grows at Lone Cone Mountain plants like the ones that helped the man to survive the flood. There is still one man alive who claims to have seen these plants.

After the flood Gnahss took pity on the people. At that time they lived at Tse-teak-wis, which is not far from Lone Cone Mountain. The people were hungry and so Gnahss allowed a dead whale to drift by. The people gathered and they carried their whaling canoes into the water. A whale meant food, oil, bones to make implements, and general festivities.

It was early morning as they approached the whale and yet it grew dark. They saw that a great whirling black cloud had descended upon the whale. Then just as their spears pierced the whale, the whale lifted for a moment and then came crashing down into the water. It appeared that huge talons had gripped the whale, powerful talons that might easily escape with this gift from Gnahss.

The people saw this black cloud, this thunderbird, posed a great threat. A threat that might mean an ever greater hunger, that might mean a slow agonizing death.

There arose from the depths of their beings a chanting prayer, a powerful, piercing prayer that seemed to anger the black cloud. Thunder rolled across the heavens and lightning flashed dangerously close but the people steadfastly chanted, beat their sticks and shook their rattles.

Again the black cloud descended on the whale and again it was forced to drop its heavy load. The black cloud seemed to grow angrier and unleashed thunder and lightning down on the people. Again the black cloud descended and again it was forced to drop the great whale. In a fury now, the cloud released gigantic hailstones. Hailstones that were many times the size of ordinary hail. Luckily the stones did not fall closely spaced but wide apart. It is said that if paddles were held broadside to the hail the paddles would splinter and become useless. And if a hailstone should hit a person on the head he would be stunned momentarily.

Time after time the black cloud descended on the great whale and still the people chanted, beat their sticks and shook their rattles. When evening came the black cloud seemed to lose spirit, to grow tired. It descended less frequently until at last it stopped altogether. Slowly the cloud moved away. It had been defeated. The people had won and this meant that there would be feasting, rejoicing and thanksgiving.

Tom and Gertie Lambert with their sons, Russell and Stuart, and their dog Ting, in front of their log cabin in 1920.

CORTES ISLAND BACK THEN

GERTIE LAMBERT

I CAME UP TO CORTES with my mother, Anna Ripple, in October of 1908. My mother was to be married for the third time, to a homesteader, Augustus Tiber of Manson's Landing. My stepsister in Vancouver had everything ready for us as we had to get up early the next morning to go to Cortes. I think my stepfather had got all the equipment we needed for the rain, umbrellas and rain test coats; back where we came from, in Minnesota, they were having snowstorms.

We sailed to Cortes on the old *Cassiar*. We had never been on a boat before; it was all new to us. Electric light and all that—we didn't even have that back home in Minnesota. We had a stateroom on the ship and four of us slept together in one room. When we arrived at Manson's Landing there was a special reception party waiting to greet us. When we saw it, we figured there were a lot of boys up there on Cortes Island, but it turned out some of the "boys" were actually girls dressed up in overalls! That same eve-

The Lamberts' goat dairy farm, 1929. A fire had gone through the valley in 1918, which made it look so bad the locals called it Paradise Valley.

ning we had a picnic supper at the picnic grounds, by the lake near Tibers'. Everybody on Cortes came to it.

I went to the first schoolhouse on Cortes, a log cabin with a Union Jack nailed to the flagpole outside. There were homemade desks inside about four or five inches wide. Believe me, you had to sit up straight in them. The Mike Manson twins, two sets of them, attended school with me, and we had a heck of a job telling them apart as they looked alike and all wore overalls. Later on my son Stuart attended school at the second schoolhouse, and the only difference was that the flag was raised every day. I can remember some of the schoolteachers: George Griffin, Miss Gorange, Mrs Patterson and Miss McBeth. After I had attended school on Cortes I went down to St Anne's Academy in Vancouver for one year. I then went back to Cortes for two months before starting work in a boarding house in Vancouver.

I met my husband, Tom Lambert, at a Cortes Island party. Everybody would walk clean across the island to get to those parties. They were called surprise parties but I think everybody knew about them. All the settlers would walk there, no matter how far it was. Nobody thought anything about the walking; it was regarded as part of the fun.

I married Tom in Vancouver on February 17, 1913, at St. Patrick's Church. All the young girls on Cortes Island got married in Vancouver. After we were married we moved back to Cortes, and by golly, the first thing I was to see when we arrived at the Lambert homestead was a pile of dishes waiting to be washed.

There was a lot of work to be done on a homestead: raising a garden, looking after animals and canning all the surplus food. Everybody had to work hard in the garden. We grew potatoes, turnips and sugar beets. Later on we had an orchard and there was fruit to pick and can. I can remember a bag of spuds selling for a dollar. It was fairly easy to get fresh meat as there were quite a few deer on Cortes—all you had to do was to go out and shoot one. We salted some of the meat but most of it we canned. We had goats, too, which Tom had bought off the Padgetts. The Padgett family were the first settlers on Cortes to have goats. We kept the does for a good milk supply; the young bucks we had for meat. Some of the settlers used to pick the clams off the beach, but we didn't bother with them too much. We always made it our business to have a month's supply of staples in, such as flour, sugar, dried beans and peas.

We all looked forward to the boat coming up three times a week to Manson's Landing. Everybody would be there, all talking and criticizing. We always had lots of fun waiting for the boat to come in—once in a while we would even pass the time by having a dance at the

The first panel truck in Powell River, 1928.

The Lamberts moved to Powell River and ran a goat dairy farm from 1926–1933.

wharf. As my half-sister Phildelma used to say, "You had to jump across the cracks when you came to them." There was usually an accordion and violins to provide the music. We would stay at the dance until daylight, and if we were cold or tired there were bales of hay to sit on. We would all have to work the next day, even though we had been up all night.

I used to go over to Padgetts' before I got married. I can remember the day I went down with Phildelma and Carl for afternoon tea. Mrs. Padgett had her silver tea set out; they were the only people on Cortes to own one, it had come all the way from England. We sat outside at tables with lace covers. We had some pictures taken too—Mrs. Padgett had a camera that took pictures on glass plates and I had a Kodak Brownie No. 2 camera. We used to develop and print our own pictures. I still have many of my original pictures, although some have grown faded with time.

Stuart Lambert, age 4, gets a haircut from his father while Grandpa looks on. 1918.

BASKETMAKING
on the Sunshine Coast

BASKETS are one of those beautiful acts of creation that have tangled beginnings. They have been found in some form in many cultures, including the native people of the Pacific Northwest, for whom basketmaking was an integral part of life. Spruce root, pine root, cedar root, willow bark, cattail stems, devil's claw fibre, split osier, grass, horsehair and hazelnut shots have all been used in the basketry of British Columbia, as have porcupine quills and feathers from the meadowlark, mallard and quail. Heated cactus and balsam poplar buds were used for sealing and yellow pine pitch for repairs. Cedar is the most abundant material in our local area and is the primary product used by the Coast Salish Indians.

Storing, transporting and cooking were the traditional uses of cedar baskets. Burden baskets, used for transporting dry materials, had a flat side so they would not roll when carried on the back. Large burden baskets were occasionally used as bathtubs and washtubs. Baskets for liquids were bowl-shaped, while those for storing small articles were shaped like nuts. Trays were used in fanning fires, playing dice games and serving food. Upon the arrival of European traders and settlers, baskets became items of sale as well.

When a basket was to be used for cooking, it was made watertight by sealing it with mashed soapberries. The berries were boiled right in the basket, and

their seeds would seep into the crevices. Today at Mount Currie in the Pemberton Valley, a substitute of sugar, flour and water made into a paste is smeared inside the basket.

I have been told of two ways to cook in a basket. The primary method is to fill it with water and then add hot stones until the water becomes hot enough to cook in. An alternative is to put food in the basket first and then throw in a red-hot stone that has had water poured on it to make it steam. As the stone cools, more steaming hot stones can be added.

Baskets were made and designed almost exclusively by women, unlike the Chilkat blankets which were woven by women from patterns drawn on boards by men.

Basket designs varied widely among communities and groups, and as the women created new patterns, they often shared them with others. An exception occurred in some groups when a pattern with an unknown meaning would come to a woman in a dream; other tribes would not copy the design until it had first been used by the dreamer's daughter or granddaughter.

In 1900, Livingston Farrand described the basketry patterns of the Salish Indians as a "process of evolution from realistic portrayal to geometric representation." A snake is a simple zigzag, vertically arranged; this vertical arrangement can also represent lightning. A horizontal zigzag can be a mountain chain. Among the Lower Thompson people were patterns said to represent mountains with lakes in the valleys, grave or burial boxes, butterfly wings and grouse tracks, together with an earth line. One pattern used by the Lillooet people showed a head with an open mouth, teeth, and hair along the back of the head; another design was intestines with a band of flies below.

Basket trading was common. In 1850, Lytton and Lower Thompson baskets were traded to the Spences Bridge and Nicola people for various items. A large burden basket could be traded for a secondhand buckskin shirt or dress or buffalo robe; ten cakes of mashed and dried berries or a large first-rate buckskin. An average-size basket brought a pair of secondhand leggings with fringe or a good doeskin. A small basket was worth a pair of secondhand leggings or a coat of Hudson's Bay cloth and a new pair of men's moccasins.

Mary Jackson, Eliza August and Ethel Julian, all of whom lived on the Sechelt Indian Reserve, described how a woman must first obtain and prepare the needed materials.

To make a cedar basket, one must dig cedar roots. The most favourable time for digging is late spring or early summer, when the sap is running. It is good if the ground is somewhat moist and not too rocky, as you often have to dig deep and for quite a distance (I was told of people digging as deep as six feet). You start digging between four and twenty feet from the base of a live tree, as the roots any nearer the base of the tree are too stiff to work with. You have to know what to look for because it can be difficult to distin-

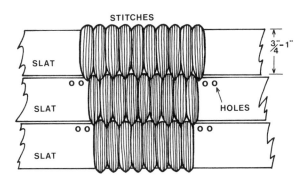

guish cedar roots from the web of living matter beneath the surface. The root can be identified by the reddish-brown colour of its bark. Then it should be tested for quality by bending it to see how much spring it has: the more spring, the better. Another test is to bite the root: if your teeth sink in, the root is good. Once you have found a good root, you start following it, pulling and digging in a direction away from the tree as far as that root will take you.

After the root is cut, the small hairs on it must be removed at once to prevent little holes from forming. Then the outer cortex of the root is scraped or split off. Some women immediately split their roots into four pieces and bundle them up for drying, while other women dry the roots first for a few days before they split them into workable size pieces (approximately 1/4" wide by 1/16" thick). Sometimes the roots can be split with your teeth.

The split roots are wrapped around a core to begin constructing a basket. In earlier times and in some areas today, bundles of short roots were used for this purpose. In the Sechelt area, another part of the cedar tree is used for the "bones" of the basket. Cedar trees, preferably young, are cut down and split along the grain into slats for the bottom and sides of the basket. Slabs are taken from the lower part of the tree where there are no knots.

The final materials needed are the barks and grasses used in making patterns. Cherry bark is used in its natural reddish state, or it is dyed black. The bark should be gathered in April or May, or it may tend to curl up. The basketmaker uses a knife to make a slit in the tree, and then the bark can be peeled off easily. The underside of the bark is scraped with a knife or stone to remove any roughness, then worked with the knife on both sides until very thin. Hold the bark tightly in one hand while the other hand gently but firmly works along the surface, and hold your thumb underneath as you work the knife along the top. As the bark is scraped, tiny powder-like pieces flake off.

To obtain a black colour, the red cherry bark is weighted down with stones in an iron pot or other pot with some form of iron in it, and soaked in water for several months. The longer the soaking time, the darker the bark will become. Putting the bark in a rusty pot and covering it with wet earth will produce the same result, as will steeping the bark in tea. In earlier times, basketmakers obtained the black colour by combining alder bark and urine, or by burying the bark in muddy deposits of vegetable matter, sometimes with added charcoal or an extract of balsam bark.

White is also used in cedar root basket patterns. When corn husks are dried in the sunlight after being dipped in hot water, they will turn whitish, a process that can take any length of time from a few days to a few weeks. A good whitening effect can also be obtained using a plant referred to as "wild straw," which can be found along the Fraser River and at Mount Currie. A similar material can be found in the Sechelt area: a wheat-like plant that is green when picked, dried until white or steamed on top of a fire, then split open and uncurled to reveal a white inner section.

Now that the materials for the basket have been collected and prepared, there remains the actual weaving. It is a difficult task to describe in words the deft actions of fingers, hands and body as they work with the quiet assurance of time and experience.

Cedar baskets have either a coiled or a slat bottom. A coiled bottom is made from bundles of cedar roots coiled from the centre and wrapped by a sewing root. Slat bottoms are worked in the same manner as slat sides. There are several ways to attach the bottom slats to the sides. A bundle of cedar roots can be used to make the connection, or the bottom and side slats can be stitched directly to one another. If the bottom slats are stitched to the middle of the first side slat, a rim is formed around the outside that keeps the bottom off the ground.

After the bottom is finished, the sides can be started. Older baskets, especially those which used bundles of roots for filler, had smaller and tighter stitches. The width of the stitch is determined by the width the sewing root was split into when it was prepared. The length of the stitch reflects the thickness of the filler

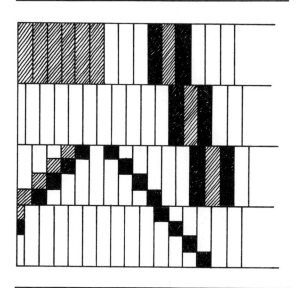

being used. Since cedar slats are 1/2" to 1 1/2" wide and root bundles are much smaller, basketmakers have found that slat baskets can be worked faster. Over time, they have proved themselves just as serviceable as the earlier styles that used root bundles for filler. Some baskets have slats for one portion and root bundles for another.

The slat can be either one circumference of the basket, or a long continuous piece. Sechelt people tend to use short pieces, while at Mount Currie a continuous upwards spiral is used. When two slats are joined, their ends are shaped with a knife so the joint will not be readily visible.

Cedar roots are always used when wet so they will remain soft and pliable. The root is taken out of a bucket of warm water, and its end is shaped with a knife into a slight point. If the root starts to dry out while being worked, it is placed back in the water. A sharp instrument like a tiny poker is used to make holes in the slats (in past times a bone awl was used for this task). The hole is made in the top of the last completed slat; then, when the next slat is added, the sewing root is poked through the hole and looped around the new slat. Then another hole is made next to the last hole

and the sewing root is poked through once again. This completes one stitch and begins the next. As each loop is completed, it is pulled tight, gradually covering the slat. (Pulling an arm's length of root can be a lot of work!) When a new root needs to be added, it is placed in the last hole made for the previous root and the ends of both roots are carefully trimmed so the stitch where they join conceals the ends.

A pattern can be worked in as the stitches are made, often by imbrication or beading (most of the local baskets I have seen were imbricated). To do imbrication, one tucks dyed or undyed cherry bark, corn husks or grasses under the stitches of the sewing root after having wrapped it around the outside. The tuck or fold allows the sewing root to hold the imbricating material in place against the core when the stitch is pulled tight. Depending on the pattern being worked, the imbricating material may be a short piece or a long strip, and may cover the entire length of the stitch or only a portion of it. A thin diagonal or vertical line might require separate pieces for each stitch, while a horizontal line would use a continuous strip of imbricating material tucked under successive stitches along a slat.

Beading is similar to plain weave because its effect arises from the pattern material being woven over and under the sewing root. Intricate patterns can be built up by using two or three pieces of pattern material. One example would be carrying one colour over and under one stitch and the other colour over and under two stitches.

The three ladies I talked with on the Sechelt Indian Reserve all had a twinkle in their eyes as they recalled memories of gathering roots. Many of these women made baskets: seven or eight women would start out early in the day, carrying mattocks and hatchets for digging and cutting, and proceed to their favourite spots. One good spot for digging was the land now occupied by St. Mary's Hospital in Sechelt. Sometimes they would take longer camping trips to places throughout the Peninsula, where they had special spots in mind for gathering. At dusk they would return, carrying huge bundles of roots. In the summer, the women often sat under shade trees, each working on a basket. A young girl could learn much about basketmaking simply by observing this, and could even assimilate enough knowledge to begin on her own. As one lady said to me, "Nothing was too hard for the women in those days."

Even the earliest baskets made by the women I spoke with were for sale or trade, often being traded for clothing and shoes in North Vancouver. By the time these women were making baskets, they no longer used them for utilitarian purposes. The women knew of no special significance attached to the patterns in their basketry, nor did they know of any ritual or ceremony involved in gathering or preparing the materials.

Mary Jackson was still making baskets on the Sechelt Indian Reserve almost until her death in the fall of 1991. Her creations and the work of other women can be seen at the Tems Swiya Museum in Sechelt.

Gathering materials remains a major problem for the women. The older women with basketmaking knowledge find it hard to dig roots, once a suitable location is found that has not been levelled for a road or subdivision. Due to various ailments, some of the women find wet cedar roots difficult to work with. At Sechelt and Mount Currie, it is the older people who are involved in the work of making baskets, and it is difficult to predict whether younger people will be willing to take their place when the time comes.

TROLLER

KEVIN ROBERTS

AN OUTRAGEOUS AVALANCHE of sea burst against the bow where Bill lay on the starboard bunk, and the boat timbers shivered and trembled the full thirty-six-foot length of the *Pacific Maid*. Mel, the skipper, had been sick for three days now and so had his son Bert, and the fish boat was barely under control. Bill lay there in his floater jacket, the rubber tailpiece drawn up between his thighs and hooked to the front. Bert had made a number of cracks about it, but as soon as the wind hit the boat past the moaning foghorn of Tofino Harbour, Bill'd put it on and left it on. This was his first trip as a deckhand on the outside and the sheer size of the Pacific disturbed him deeply. Two bad seasons on the inside, no sockeye, no pinks, and his small fish boat had been claimed by the Royal Bank. He'd had no choice but to find a job, start again at the bottom, as a deckhand on a large Pacific troller. And he was lucky to get on with Mel, he knew. But somehow he felt he didn't want to be here.

He was stunned on that first day out when Mel had confessed that he was always seasick for the first couple of days, and sometimes for longer in bad weather. It seemed crazy, even dangerous to put yourself into a job where you suffered so much, where control over your body was in such jeopardy. But, Mel had added, seasickness was a lot more common than most fishermen admitted. Greed and pride kept them at it, that and the strange attraction the sea had for some men. That was the hardest to believe.

Above him, outside in the dark, the wind thrummed on the wires of the poles like a mad guitarist. Beside him, on the other bunk, Bert moaned gently, and above and behind him, Mel lay suffering in the wheelhouse bunk. The gale rose and fell in sixty-mile-an-hour bursts, and he was glad he could not see the swells, topped with flying white lace, that rolled ominously and endlessly from the heart of the dark Pacific.

Four days ago, they'd smashed and rolled their way fifty miles out from Tofino, the weather channel predicting falling winds and sea. They'd fished that first morning, their thighs braced hard against the sides of the fish well in the stern, slapping the gurdies in on only half the lines because the yawing, pitching boat could not be held straight, even on the Wagner autopilot. It was a monstrously unstable world, where the sky swung like a mad chandelier, and at the bottom of a swell, the boat seemed totally surrounded by the seething grey sea. He had not realized how totally encased in the pitching bowl of the Pacific they were, until they encountered another fish boat, the *Ocean Rambler*, about the same size, and its toy-like struggle to lift up from the weight of the sea made him fear that this other frail cockle of wood might not rise this time, or the next.

They had caught fish that first day, coho and a few medium springs, but the big fish broke the lines or ran amok about the barely controllable boat. He had brought one spring alongside, thirty pounds, maybe more, and he swung the gaff down and into its head, but the boat yawed, and the gaff and fish were pulled beyond his strength and he let go before he too was tipped into the maelstrom. The skipper's curses were torn from his lips by the wind as he came aft in a running crouch, shouldered him aside and with huge hands, crisscrossed with the white scars of nylon fish-line, manhandled the flapping spring with the gaff still in its head into the chequers and expertly killed it with a single blow behind the head.

He was embarrassed, though he could not hear Bert's jibes from the other side of the boat, but not for long, when the skipper, with a sudden lurch, pushed by him again, green-faced, and vomited into the spume. Bert soon followed his father and for what seemed an endless time, both of them leaned over the side and vomited time and time again.

It was then that he'd taken charge, scuttled to the wheelhouse to adjust the Wagner, crouched and run back to run the lines, pull the salmon, run out the lines again, cleaned the fish and stacked them in the chequers. But the wind and sea grew and the main line and the deep line on the starboard side crossed and tangled and for half an hour he struggled to bring both

of them in and clear the gear. The skipper watched, red-eyed, and finally told him to pull all the lines in and lash them down.

Though the skipper stopped regularly to retch overboard, Mel worked with him until all the gear was on board and the lines and lead cannonballs lashed down.

Together they pulled the prostrate Bert into the wheelhouse and down into the bunk. Bill went out again to the stern, staggered back with armful after armful of salmon, crawled deep down into the hold of the boat, a dark icy womb, stuffed ice into the cleaned bellies of the fish and stacked them into the waiting ice. Then, half-crouching, he staggered back into the cabin.

"Sea-anchor, Bill," mumbled Mel, pointing to the bow, "I'll run the boat up, you drop it." This was real danger. The weighted parachute with the red Scotsman buoy had to be eased overboard so it sank and opened deep beneath the sea. With this down the boat rode easily, moving with the tide a mile or so in and out, on the ballooned tension of the underwater anchor. But it was dangerous to put out in a high wind. If the chute snapped open in the gale the rope would whip out like a snake striking. If the boat was not held tight against the smashing swell, the rope jerked about and the feet and body of the man, already threatened by the great wash of water pounding against it, could be washed overboard. The very idea of walking out to where the grey sea bounded onto the bow was almost too much for him, except for the haggard look of the skipper, white-faced and red-eyed. He knew then that he had to do it, not just for them on the boat, but for himself, because the sea was building relentlessly and it was doubtful if they could turn and run safely before it back to Tofino.

And he had shuffled grimly out along the deck, gripping the handrail tightly with both gloved hands, past the wheelhouse and out onto the bow. There the first burst of swell knocked him soaking and breathless to his knees. Worse, the suck of the sea off the deck rushed about him and loosened his footing. In the second or two before the next wrestling wave burst upon him he worked with one hand on the lashed parachute. Quickly, he timed his work so that in the brief dip of the bow, before the next swell deluged him, the parachute and its chain and rope were freed. He hooked one foot about a stanchion, braced the other, and in the same two-second dip, let the parachute slip steadily through his gloved left hand over the side.

It was not classic seamanship. There were many men of the West Coast fishing fleet for whom this act was daily bread, but for him, the final "tung" of the rope tight against the capstan, the red Scotsman floating before the boat now easing back, was a gong of triumph. He sat, hanging onto the rail, his knees braced against the stanchion, totally exhausted, wet through, and not at all jubilant. He thought of the poached salmon steaks he'd seen once for an exorbitant price, served in silver chafers in a restaurant on Sloane Square in London, and the enormity of the callous

economics of it made him burst out with crazy laughter. Eventually, he crawled back on his knees, gripping the rail, and got into the wheelhouse.

He told himself through clenched teeth that this was it, that never again would he risk the plunge and certain death in that cold and bitter sea. It was over. He'd get a shore job, pumping gas, unloading fish, anything to avoid this pulse and roll of madness of the sea.

The skipper sat with his head down on the wheel, and Bill crawled past him and down into the bunk next to Bert. The boat now rode more easily, tossing like a massive child whose fever has broken, and even though the sea still smashed and burst against the hull he fell quickly asleep. He dreamed he was in a strange moving bed with a beautiful green woman who undulated and moved under and away from him every time he tried to possess her.

A strange, rumbling sound growing nearer brought him to wakefulness, and he got up unsteadily, his limbs rigid with cold, and stepped up into the wheelhouse. Mel lay asleep on the wheelhouse couch, his white face garish every second or two from the flash of the strobe light on the mast top. The sea was unabated. Green frills ran constantly up and down the wheelhouse window, obscuring the bow light. On the port bow half a mile and closing, at the tops of the massive swells, he could see a row of lights in the whirling darkness. He fervently hoped the radar operator on the freighter out there was awake and that the many blips of the fishing fleet tossing at anchor were clear in the stormy night. The freighter passed quickly, unperturbed it seemed by the muscular walls of water in which it moved. He wished then, as many fishermen have, for a boat so big the sea could not threaten. He thought, too, of the wreaths rotting on the Anglican Church wharf at Bamfield, and the inscription, "O Lord your sea is so strong, and our boat is so frail."

He looked about him at the unutterable darkness, the wild wind and crashing sea and felt a great loneliness, until, in the distance, the quick flash of a tiny strobe appeared, another fish boat, anchored too in this hissing vortex, and another flash, and another, and suddenly all about, at the top of the swells, the flick, flick, miles away, here and there, magical in the madness of the tossing storm. It was strangely and utterly comforting. These little lights, the community of faith, flickering, miles away from home and warmth and safety, the lights of the boats of the West Coast fishing fleet, held by the flowers of their sea anchors, keeping faith with each other, and this arduous endeavour upon the encircling sea.

Flying Eyes

DENNIS CURRIE

Today I flew a logger into camp
And I watched as he looked at the trees
Then I picked up a fisherman coming back
And together we watched the sea

I've seen truckers watch the road below
And yachtsmen see the boats
Tourists get first impressions
And beachcombers look for floats

Ecologists spot the estuaries
Canoeists look for tributaries
My friends look for their homes

Log buyers see the log booms
Fast at fifty feet
Store owners see the town below
And pick a busy street

Some people love the mountains
Some just watch the seagulls
Skiers see the secluded slopes
And sharp eyes catch the eagles

Prospectors scan the rock bluffs
Private pilots watch the dials
Some folks don't like flying at all
Some are just all smiles

Hunters check for flocks of birds
Surfers catch a curl
Climbers scan the peaks above
And I see all the world

Sky Dancer

DENNIS CURRIE

I buzzed a freighter
I could smell it
As I flew low at its stern
The smell of the galley
Like a downtown shoreline alley
And the diesel that freighters all burn

There was no one on deck
As I passed her
But I saw the mate on the bridge look at me
Then a tangle of masts
And then as the bow passed
I was alone with the sea

Dennis

DENNIS CURRIE

Black float bottoms in the sun
An airplane in the water below

From way up here, it's very clear
But my heart is crying no

Hurry Doc, let's get down there
And see if some survived

Sorry Den, but it's too late
There's no one left alive

It's like a war that no one fought
Though we lost it in the end

My God Dennis, there were three of us
And one of us is dead

Eagle

DENNIS CURRIE

After I killed the Eagle in the 185
I thought I had lost my touch
I'm past middle age and took it to heart
But I know that I worry too much

So I took this job I don't do it for money
Of that I have little need
But I wanted to fly as a friend with the eagles
That's my personal greed

To take that bird's life was not my intention
Though my avoidance maneuver was lame
He chose to attack the perceived aggressor
Lucky for me our fates weren't the same

Days later his sister took my best rabbit
In a way it was an eye for an eye
As I told the kids that's God's reason for bunnies
I killed the eagle in a small part of the sky

THE SACRAMENTAL DANCE
✳ of the TWO OLD LOGGERS

by JOHN SHREIBER

For Jack Fraser—wherever he may be

ON AN OVERTIME SATURDAY MORNING with the air gentle from an early autumn rain, two old loggers saw each other across the length of the landing. They had not seen each other for a long time and there were reconnections to make and news to share. The crews had begun their coffee and smokes, but the two old loggers, with no obvious advance gestures of intention, turned instead and began the slow, shambling walk, caulks crunching, to the centre of the landing where the newly moved yarder and the just-raised spar tree stood. The Finn, short, stocky, solid, reached the centre point first and, thumbs hooked under his Police suspenders, waited in the shadow of the spar. The other man, older, stiffer, body shrunken inside his shapeless denim work pants, joined him and in tandem now, the two carefully eased reluctant leg joints into squatting positions on the fresh gravel and sharp-edged yellow cedar chips. Each man, one knee lower, elbows firmly planted, hands dangling, faces the other. Above, the spar tree towers, dark against the sky.

The one logger, having stuck his work gloves in rear pocket, clears with thumb the morning's snoose-wad from his lip and few lower teeth, turning aside to spit out the last black remnants. The other, the Finn, clears his throat in commiseration and reaches under his grey Stanfields top into the breast pocket of his shirt for his sack of makings. He begins the deft business of extracting the flimsy paper from its orange package and placing it on his palm with one hand, and reaching in, laying out, and arranging the thick pinch of Player's Fine Cut with the fingers of the other. Passing the makings to the waiting older man, he rolls the works of his own with fingers of both hands into the perfect cylinder and finishes off with a concluding swipe of the tongue to seal his effort.

While the second old logger repeats the exercise with the same thick-fingered dexterity and sequence, the first, the Finn, sticks his handiwork into one corner of his lips and again reaches under his Stanfields, feeling the other breast pocket for matches. Producing one from a crushed box, he strikes it with sudden violence on the fly zipper of his work jeans, then swiftly moves the burst of sulphurous flame to the patient cigarette-end of his partner. The old man curls his hands over the cupped hands of the Finn against a possible breeze, sucks in the first igniting inhalation, then adjusts his hands slightly to help the other culminate his part of the ritual.

For a second there is no motion between the two old loggers hunkered on the gravel but for pulled flame in folded hands. Task accomplished, the Finn, with a twitch of the fingers, flicks his match through damp air in an arc of fine blue smoke to the ground. Both men pause, then pull a long hard drag and hold it briefly while chips, gravel, yarder and spar tree shift abruptly to one side, stop and hold, for one bright, suspended, ineffable moment, then return in equilibrium. The two old loggers exhale gratefully, slowly, squinty-eyed in clouds of smoke.

The one, passing his glance, so as to meet, briefly, his partner's eyes, and following through to rest his gaze on a point somewhere beyond the other's shoulder, begins a second slow drag. Head shrouded in fresh white smoke, eyes slitted, the partner returns the look, longer this time, drawing the pupils back to him.

"Yessir," he says.

The first logger, eyes now cast on the ground, nods.

The two men squatting at the foot of the spar tree finish their smokes in silence.

A breeze, having stayed itself in seeming patience, now stirs, and the passline, a light strawline, flaps absently a little, rhythmic against the massive trunk of the spar. At the top of the tree, one hundred feet above the ground, above the newly hung and strung bull block and haulback block, guylines reach, taut as knife edges, out to the four directions.

One of the resting crews, looking up and seeing the two oldtimers under the spar tree says, "Look at them two old fuckers! Would you believe, back in the thirties, they were two of the fastest high riggers on the en-tire coast?"

The others, jaws slowly working, shake their heads in doubt, wondering at the sheer inconceivability of the idea. Dragging busily on their tailor-mades, they resume, like crows, their coffee-break chatter.

FIRE ❧ IN A FINNISH COLONY SOINTULA ❧ 1903 ❧

PAULA WILD

THE TAILOR was the first to smell the smoke. Shortly after 8:00 p.m. on Thursday, January 29, 1903, his shout of "Fire!" halted the meeting of the Kalevan Kansa Colonization Company. Fifty members of the Finnish colony had gathered on the third floor of the communal hall to discuss their financial situation.

A year and a month had passed since the Finns had established their utopian society on Malcolm Island, four miles off the northeast corner of Vancouver Island. From all parts of the world, Finlanders with a variety of backgrounds and occupations had come to the small island seeking freedom of language and of religious beliefs, as well as economic security. To the

Kalevan Kansa Colonization Company Board of Directors, Sointula, 1904.

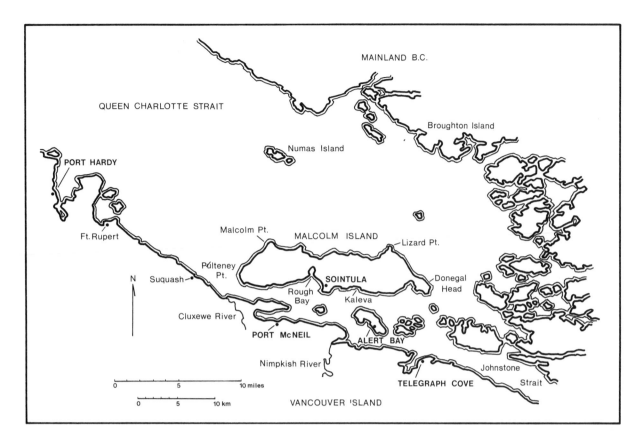

Finns, emigration seemed to be the only means of escaping the oppression of the Russian tsar and the Finnish church, but on Vancouver Island, where many first settled, they found a different type of tyranny in the dangerous and low-paying coal mines of James Dunsmuir. To realize their dreams of new world freedom, a group of Finnish immigrants in Nanaimo formed a utopian society where work, meals and property would be shared on a communal basis.

On November 27, 1901, the secretary of the British Columbia Bureau of Information and Immigration, R. Edward Gosnell, signed an agreement with the Kalevan Kansa Colonization Company, agreeing that in seven years, providing that certain conditions were met and improvements made, title to the 28,000 acres of Malcolm Island would be granted to the Finns. The Finns named their new settlement Sointula, or Harmony, and to assist them in their struggle to convert the raw wilderness into utopian reality, Matti Kurikka, a political activist and charismatic visionary, was brought from Australia to be their leader.

Born in 1863, Kurikka grew up in Ingria, a part of Finland alternately dominated by Sweden and Russia. While he was attending the University of Helsinki, Kurikka's discontent with the establishment led him to search for alternatives in philosophical and political idealism. By the age of twenty- three he had started his own newspaper and had earned a reputation for being critical of the ruling hierarchy, especially the narrow-minded control of the church, and for being an ardent supporter of the labour movement.

Eventually Kurikka became a prominent member of the Finnish Socialist Party, but when young Marxist radicals organized against him and the tsar accelerated Russification of Finland, he began to campaign for emigration as the only means to realize an ideal society. Late in 1899, accompanied by 180 Finns, he left for Queensland, Australia, where he planned to establish a utopian commune. When the Australian government's promise of financial support proved to be more of a bid for cheap labour for their sugar cane fields, Kurikka organized a contract to construct railway sleepers near Chillagoe. Not long into the contract the Finns felt that they were being cheated on their wages, and as their leader, Kurikka was held responsible. Other jobs offering 12 shillings a week soon lured the men away, and Kurikka's utopia never got further than ten tents pitched near the railway track. Kurikka was alone, destitute and ill when the invitation to travel to British Columbia arrived.

Life in the new utopia of Sointula was primitive, but there was no shortage of energy and enthusiasm. What was lacking, however, was capital, and to raise money, a joint-stock company was formed with membership shares of $200 per adult. Few of the Finns had the financial resources to purchase their shares outright. Some made a down payment of $50, while many pledged to work off their debt. Kurikka was advertising Sointula as a thriving communal colony when in reality it was a heavily forested island requiring extensive manual clearing. Many who came to the island were tailors, cobblers and other city tradesmen, ill-equipped for the task at hand.

It was soon obvious that it would be some time before farming, logging or any other industry would generate any revenue. From the outset the Kalevan Kansa was forced to obtain loans for even the basics of food, clothing and tools. The Finns established *The Aika* (Time), Canada's first Finnish American newspaper, and through it Kurikka publicized more of his idealistic plans for the commune, giving little thought to their practical application. His attacks against the church became so venomous that threats were made against his life. He said that he felt "like a fierce unmanageable train engineer who needed someone to act as brakeman when the velocity became too high." He asked the Kalevan Kansa to send to Finland for Austin Makela, "his best and most trusted friend." Kurikka felt that Makela, a fellow student at the University of Helsinki and newspaper co-worker in Finland, could act as his brakeman. Even he realized that his rampant idealism required tempering with Makela's steady sense of practicality.

The fall of 1902 found over two hundred people living in Sointula, and to house the overflow a three-story structure was built. The top floor was designated as a meeting room and temporary tailor shop, and the two lower floors were divided by 72-foot-long halls with sleeping rooms on each side. The building was hastily constructed out of green lumber which soon shrank, leaving large cracks in the walls and floors. Sound slipped easily through these crevices and the communal house was nicknamed "Melula" (Noisy).

The entire colony was living on credit, and as president it was Kurikka's responsibility to procure it. He freely admitted using his powers of persuasion to stretch the truth and by January 1903, the colony's creditors were suspicious. A trustee, J.W. Bell, was sent to assess the situation. Bell was resting in his room on the ground floor of Melula when the tailor shouted, "Fire!"

On the third floor Kurikka quickly ordered everyone to follow him out of the building while Makela, now secretary of the Kalevan Kansa, directed people to form an orderly line at the head of the stairs. In addition to the fifty people present at the meeting, fifty-three others, predominantly women and children, were in the sleeping rooms below. When Kurikka reached the ground floor and opened the door to the hall, he was forced backwards by a great blast of dense, hot smoke. He pushed his way outside, men, women and children flowing down the long, winding stairway behind him. Smoke billowed from the rear of the ground floor hall and the thin board partitions erupted in flame.

In an interview with the *Vancouver Daily Province* on February 9, 1903, Kurikka said, "By the time I reached the outside of the building, men and women

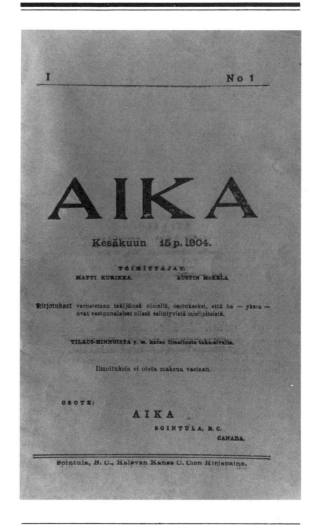

were throwing children out of the second storey windows and jumping after them." Bell reported to the newspaper that "the fire was the quickest I ever saw. I stood with other men under a window catching children as they were handed out and dropped from upper windows. The smoke and flames seemed to burst from every opening at once, making it almost impossible to enter the hall. People leaped headlong through the windows—one fellow threw himself through space, coming out with a cloud of smoke and crashing his face and shoulders against the ground below. Women jumped with their clothing on fire and their hair burning."

Mrs. Oberg was in one of the sleeping rooms on the ground floor when the fire broke out. She carried her two young sons outside, then found herself unable to re-enter the building. When her husband August escaped from the third floor and heard that his two daughters were still inside, he immediately plunged back into the flames. Finding the little girls huddled in bed he picked them up and started for the door. The floor collapsed beneath him when they were halfway

Matti Kurikka, Finland, 1899.

to safety. As he fell, Elma and Hilma slipped from his arms and were lost. Oberg struggled to the door with his clothes, face and hands on fire and was pulled out of the building by several men. The bodies of the girls were later found no more than four feet from the door.

Meanwhile, on the second storey of the building, an engineer for the colony named Heinonen panicked. He grabbed his buddy, a bricklayer named Wallin, and begged him not to leave without him. Unfortunately,

Heinonen's desperate grip prevented both men from moving. They swayed in the smoke, Wallin struggling to escape, and Heinonen struggling to hang on. Those on the ground watched the drama through the second storey windows, where first it appeared that Wallin was in control, then it seemed that Heinonen was. Some thought that Wallin, who had "the strength of an ox," would conquer Heinonen; others thought that both men would die.

Sointula cemetery. Gravestone for the eleven who died in the January 29, 1903 fire.

"Finally after what seemed an age," Kurikka recalled, "and just when the flames were licking their way through the open window, Wallin was seen by a mighty effort to raise the now thoroughly insane engineer to the sill, and a moment later both men tumbled to the ground terribly burned."

Within six minutes of the tailor's shout the interior of the hall was red with flame and filled with a heat so intense that it blistered the skin from a distance of fifteen feet. Women and children on the ground floor were cut off from the outside door. A few of the rooms had no windows, while others had openings too small to push even a child through. Maria Hantula, a recent emigrant from Dakota, had rescued two of her children and returned for the remaining four. She was found dead, crouched over her three children with the baby in her arms. Maria Lofbacka and her two children, Tekla and Oiva, died in a similar manner.

In one hour Melula was destroyed. The residence of Dr. Oswald Beckman, the colony physician, became the headquarters for the injured. These included the blacksmith Lingren Nygren, who was severely burned and had injured his back jumping from the third floor, Austin Makela, badly burned on the face and hands and unable to see, a woman who had jumped from the second storey and landed on her head, and a score of others, seriously bruised and burned.

Bell gave the *Vancouver Daily Province* this account of the next morning: "Looming up through the blackened debris were the remains of the stoves, iron bedsteads, and the metal portions of sewing machines. Then we tried to find out how many were lost, and the number grew from five to eleven in all. To add to the discomfort a high wind was blowing and with it came sleet and rain. There was no place for anyone to go outside of the rooms of the doctor's house and these were crowded with the injured. Under an iron bedstead I found a human skull, and a few feet from it was a baby's body all shrivelled up.

"A woman came hurrying up, just as I was trying to get the body of the baby. I asked her if she had lost anyone in the fire. She announced something about not understanding English, and then, with a wail in her voice she said, 'Baby, baby,' and pointed to the steaming ruins. I could not do or say anything. She put her apron to her eyes and a moment later had gone."

In addition to the dead and injured, all of the colony's precious supplies, which had been stored in Melula, had been destroyed. Those who had lived in the building were destitute as well as homeless, and many of the women and children had only their nightclothes to wear. Damages were estimated in excess of $10,000. On Saturday the first relief arrived from Alert Bay on nearby Cormorant Island, and Kurikka and Bell travelled to Vancouver to seek further assistance.

As there was no coroner in the area, William Halliday, Justice of the Peace in Alert Bay, formed a jury of six men to look into the tragedy. The jury's terse verdict stated "that the said parties came to their death by fire and that the said fire was accidental." They did not determine the exact cause of the fire, but the residents of Sointula had their own ideas.

On the first floor and at the rear of Melula there had been a large oven that was used to bake goods for the colony. Hot air pipes ran from the oven down the halls, with smaller pipes branching into individual rooms to provide heat. Some of these flues were metal but many were fashioned from wood. Several people thought that a blast of hot air had blown over a lamp and started the fire. Others felt that the heating system itself was the culprit: with hot pipes igniting dry wood, there was ample ventilation in Melula to fan a stray spark. Even darker speculations began to circulate. It was said that Bell had been sent by the government to examine the Kalevan Kansa Colonization Company books. There was talk of embezzlement, and even accusations that Kurikka, as president, and Oberg, as treasurer, had burned the building deliberately to destroy the company ledger.

Tension strained the commune until a special meeting was called to deal with the matter. Kurikka demanded that the primary slanderers have their memberships cancelled. The two men in question had already left the island, and the majority of the colony was against their memberships. A debate took place and in the heat of the moment Kurikka threatened to resign and leave the island. In the interests of restoring

Sointula, c. 1904.

harmony, the board agreed to Kurikka's motion. Makela, who had regained his eyesight, strongly opposed this decision, and the two men faced the first serious conflict in their friendship.

The flames that devoured Melula provided fuel for an irreversible undercurrent of dissension and distrust. Monetary difficulties were a primary concern, and in an attempt to bolster the commune's finances, Kurikka placed a bid on the construction of bridges over the Capilano and North Seymour rivers in Vancouver. He was awarded the contract but the colony members felt that the bid was underestimated. Kurikka argued that the contract was a stepping-stone to further work in Vancouver and that they would forfeit the $150 deposit if they dishonoured the contract. As usual, Kurikka got his way, but once work began, it soon became apparent that no allowance had been made for foundations, and very little for bolts and nails. In the end, over one hundred members of the colony worked for more than four months without wages, and instead of making money, the colony incurred additional debts. Just as devastating was the loss of thousands of board feet of Malcolm Island's best timber used to construct the bridges.

The rift between Kurikka and Makela refused to mend and increasingly the two men found themselves on opposite ends of argument. The clash of their divergent philosophies came to a climax on the subject of sexual relations outside of marriage. Kurikka advocated responsible freedom in the area of sexual relations and felt that a man and a woman could live together without marriage as long as they loved each other. Makela, and most of the married members of the commune, strongly objected to the implications of free love and worried that rumours of this lifestyle would jeopardize the Finns being granted title to Malcolm Island. Hostilities became so intense that a special meeting was called to resolve the issue once and for all. Kurikka, feeling that his position was threatened, resigned and left the island, taking almost half the settlers with him.

The thirty-six families that remained on the island were left with an enormous debt and a greatly reduced labour pool. They struggled along under Makela's guidance, and he eventually suggested that the colony make fifty-year leases on eighty-acre parcels of land to protect their interests. The community was forced to liquidate the Kalevan Kansa Colonization Company, and Makela secured a government loan to discharge the colony's debts on condition that the government's previous agreement to give title to Malcolm Island to the Finns become void. The Kalevan Kansa and the Finns' dream of a socialist utopia ceased to exist on May 27, 1905. Every person on the island received ten pounds of flour, one pound of pork, a few fish, a plate, a cup and a saucer.

The end of the Kalevan Kansa Colonization Company, however, was not the end of Sointula. Many of the Finns found employment in the west coast's growing logging and fishing industries, and slowly the community grew. Today, Sointula is a prosperous fishing village and descendants of the original settlers still fish the waters and farm the soil. Echoes of their ancestors' dreams are heard in the Finnish language that is still spoken and felt in the strong sense of community spirit.

Flying for the Sake of Flying

MAURICE MCGREGOR, AS TOLD TO PAUL STODDART

I WAS BORN IN VICTORIA on May 11, 1911 and had my early schooling there, and with the great Lindbergh flight I was attracted to the romance and adventure of flying. My parents were not in favour at first, and many of their friends could not understand them permitting a youth to engage in such an impossible profession. They all thought there was no future in aviation, that it would never amount to anything. My parents said, however, "All right, if that's what he wants to do, fine."

They provided the funds for me to take lessons from BC Airways and Hal Wilson, one of the finest instructors in the country. He was very thorough and strict, which is as it should be.

On my first day he put me in the rear seat of an Eaglerock, powered by a Curtis 0X5 First World War engine, not noted for its reliability. They frequently stopped, with ensuing forced landings. Hal demonstrated the controls—it was a great sensation, and I developed a keen interest in flying for the sake of flying. As I gained experience, I realized that this was a business ideally suited for me because it offered adventure and required skills that I could develop.

BC Airways went broke when they lost a Ford Tri-Motor off Port Dungeness, so Hal Wilson was out of a job. He went to work instructing with the BC Aero Club. I followed him and we operated from a little strip on Lulu Island. I finished my training and passed all my exams, but had to wait six months for my licence because I was too young. You had to be eighteen. Once I finally obtained my licence, I went barnstorming around the province.

Economic conditions were terrible. It was very difficult to find people with enough money for lessons or a joyride; nevertheless, many of them gladly reached for their last dime. We tried to eke out a living flying out of Vancouver and Ladner, from Grauer's field, named for the Grauer family, well-known farmers in the area.

That field was the start of Rosco Turner's flight—the first nonstop flight from Vancouver to Tijuana. It was a promotion for Gilmore Gas. They advertised on the radio that "The Gilmore Lion roars!" so Turner had a lion cub with him.

Turner was a colourful character, and I remember he was a good pilot and a great showman. He wore Bedford cords riding breeches, beautiful shiny riding boots, a robin's egg blue tunic of his own design with many wings on it and "R.T." in the middle, and a Sam Browne belt. He took the lion down to the old Hotel Vancouver and fed it raw meat, which created quite a stir.

I came back to Victoria and taught flying as well as putting on displays of aerobatics and all that sort of thing. I'd storm out of James Seed Farm in Duncan and teach people up there, then I'd fly over to Saltspring Island and use the golf course. (It was a very small golf course.)

But business was slow, so I decided to drum some up in Sidney. I selected a farmer's field and put on a show to create a little excitement, then dove down onto the field. A lot of curious people showed up to see what was going on. They were the unsuspecting clients, our customers.

You'd keep moving around, trying to pick up a dollar here and a dollar there. Sometimes you'd carry passengers for a cent a pound. If the person was light they'd get a reasonable ride, but with a heavier person you'd just take off, make a quick circuit, come down again and get the next one.

I used a Fleet bi-plane, a Berling, which is a low-winged mono-plane, and a Gypsy Moth. In addition, the Sprott-Shaw school had an aviation division with an antiquated 1910 Wako 10 with a World War One engine that was always stopping, so you had to find a field to land in.

I did that for about a year with charter flights to Seattle and other places. Some character would phone up in the middle of the night after having been on a big party and would want to charter a plane, so we'd take off at dawn and charge him $35.

When I came back from Vancouver, I established my own flying school called Vancouver Island Airways. I lined up a number of students and got a fairly intensive training program under way. The residents of the area, around Uplands, complained bitterly about this airplane, this single airplane, awakening their sleeping children in the afternoon. A great campaign took place to have me cease and desist, and they managed to get the airport closed.

W.T. Straith, a Victoria lawyer and alderman, organized a committee to establish an airport at Gordon Head, now the site of the University of Victoria, so we did some flying there and operated the school.

I gave flight training to many Chinese people. As a result of this I made contact with the Chinese air force in Canton, who were looking for westerners to help train their nationals to repel the Japanese invaders. I completed negotiations with the Chinese, obtained my passport and booked my passage. I had letters of introduction to prominent Chinese cabinet ministers, including the brother of Madame Chiang Kai Shek.

When I had all my plans firmly made, I received a telegram from the RCAF headquarters informing me that an application I had made for navigation, night flying and instrument flying courses had been accepted and I was to begin immediately. I went to Camp Borden and completed the courses, and then Prime Minister R.B. Bennett cut back on aviation across the country. Canada was in such a severe financial situation that the government decided air transport was not vital, and they could not afford it.

A large number of people laid off from the air force volunteered to take a squadron of Boeing fighters to China for active combat. The government of the day would not allow this and refused to issue passports to the group.

One of the most important reasons young pilots wanted to go to China was for the employment opportunities. At home, we had to compete with more experienced World War One pilots – it was a tough, competitive situation and very difficult to earn a living.

Later, in '33, I had the opportunity of joining Canadian Airways. I was assigned to the fishery patrol based at Alert Bay to cover the south end of Vancouver Island and Knight Inlet. We had to fly with visual reference to the water, and if the ceiling and the visibility got too low we would fly close to the waves in the landing position and steer courses to various known points or lighthouses. If the visibility was too bad but the sea was smooth, we would land along the step at 60 mph.

That year the pilchards did not appear. Pilchards were herring-like fish that were very important to the oil reduction plants on the west coast, and that many fishermen depended on for their livelihood. So when they did not appear. there was great concern on the part of the industry. The Federal Fisheries Department asked us to undertake a search on the Pacific to try to locate them. Because there was no radio in the aircraft we got empty bottles in which we could put messages. I told them we would fly a hundred miles out, then make sweeps on dead reckoning, parallel to the coast, and gradually work our way in.

There were many forest fires at the time, and the visibility was bad even a hundred miles out because of all the smoke. Still, we managed eventually to find the pilchards. We estimated their position, wrote down the course to steer by and put the messages in bottles. We then found the fleet and dropped the bottles in the ocean. The fishermen retrieved the messages and steered a course for the fish.

One day Bill Jeckle, an engineer, and I were sent to McKay Lake on the Alaska Border at Burrs Bay, to pick up freight. We were flying a Fokker GCAIZ, of 1928 vintage, powered by a Wright 220 engine. It was underpowered and given to frequent mechanical difficulties, which necessitated forced landings. In hauling freight out of Hyder or Steward, this aircraft's performance was so limited it was necessary to head it into the mountains and pick up the updrafts, to gain enough altitude to pass over the Salmon Glacier. The glacier rose from Hyder nor'westward toward the Grand Yukon operation, Summit Lake, Tide Lake, and then down the Iskut River. If we got into the Iskut we could stagger along and avoid the higher mountains.

Taking off from this lake, three or four thousand feet above sea level, with a load, was a problem. We could only get airborne near the end of the lake where there was a narrow, U-shaped gut, and we had to put the aircraft on its side to get through the gut. There was a sheer drop down into Burrs Bay, so one gained speed as one went down the mountainside. That was a hair-raising situation.

When this job was completed Bill and I were instructed to proceed to Alert Bay to carry out other duties. This aircraft had been flown on the prairies and in the North where there is no rain, and magnetos were exposed to the slipstream and not covered as they should have been. Here we were, flying in a very heavy rainstorm from Alaska to Bella Bella to refuel, and just a few feet off the water. Suddenly the engine began to miss, and finally it ceased to propel the aircraft. We landed and began to drift. The water was smooth at first, but then a front went through, producing a sou'easter that almost turned the aircraft over. One wing was first under water, then the next.

We knew we could easily capsize. To avoid it, we used our sleeping bags as a sea anchor to head us into the wind. Through the rain we could see a sharp rocky promontory with a great deal of driftwood piled up against it. We could also see that the aircraft was going to pile up on the same rocks.

Fortunately, within the framework of the driftwood and jutting out at right angles was a long cedar tree with limbs on it. We steered for this with our paddles and made fast to one side. In order to secure the plane against the severity of the wind, I took a line and dove overboard, and swam across to another. We finally made the aircraft secure but realized we'd have to get out of this place, because if this storm continued we'd lose the aircraft. Jobs were very hard to come by and we were naturally very much concerned.

We climbed a small mountain just to the nor'nor'east of our location and tried to attract attention. There was a fish packer in a fiord on the other side, and we fired some shots across his bow to try to alert him. That was rather foolish, of course, because how could he hear the shots of a rifle with a gale howling? The only solution would be to place a shot directly in the pilot-house.

We returned to the aircraft and the storm subsided. The sea was calm. We thought, "let's get out this place!" We each got on a pontoon with a paddle and started paddling, not knowing where we were. We got around the point and turned up toward an inlet and kept

A Waco 10, used by the Sprott Shaw flying training school, c. 1928.

The Alaska-Washington Airways of BC's Fairchild 71, CF-AJP.

paddling for about three hours. Night was falling when finally we saw a fish boat. We were able to attract the fisherman's attention with our rifle shots, and he towed us into a cannery.

We then had to find a means of drying out the magnetos so we could continue. We removed them and put them in the cookhouse oven, dried them out, replaced them, got the engines running again and away we went. That took about two days. We got some naphtha lamp gas for fuel at the cannery, but we wanted aviation gas, so we headed for Bella Bella and then went south.

After freeze-up I took the aircraft to Kenora and began hauling fish—pickerel and pike—that came from various lakes in the north. It was transported from Kenora to Chicago, then moved by rail to New York and other markets. I was flying south to Kenora with a cargo of fish when I ran into a particularly severe snowstorm that forced me to land near Dryden. As there was only a small shack, I had to use it overnight, but I was worried about the fish freezing so I covered them with my sleeping bag. I didn't want to lose my cargo and be chastised by my superiors.

On another occasion, I was asked to transport two trappers together with all their equipment, rifles, snowshoes and everything else necessary to sustain life in the bush, including fourteen very strong huskies. They were going to their camp far north of Kenora. Some of the gear was loaded, then the huskies, then more gear and finally the trappers were wedged against the ceiling of the aircraft. When we had them battened down we closed the door of the cabin. I entered the cockpit by the exterior ladder and off we went.

We encountered a pretty heavy snowstorm with a lot of turbulence that threw the aircraft around violently. As we progressed I noticed a great stench, which had various types of odour connected with it—including, I thought, blood. Upon landing I left the cockpit and opened the door of the cabin. I was bowled over by snarling huskies, some with blood-smeared faces. Apparently they had begun fighting during the turbulence, and somehow two of them had dislodged their muzzles. The poor trappers were ashen and ill, the cabin was a shambles and the huskies continued to fight outside the plane.

HOW RAVEN CAPTURED THE DAY

RICHARD ATLEO

AT ONE TIME only half the world ever had light. In one half across the waters a chief owned the light of day. He kept the day carefully guarded in a box.

On the other side many people lived in darkness and they soon grew tired of it. They wondered what to do. Raven, who was often full of ideas, suggested that they try to capture the day from the chief who owned it. "How can we do that?" he was asked.

"We will entertain the chief with a dance. Deer, who can not only run fast but can also leap far, will dance. If we are to capture the day Deer must dance as he has never danced before. He must dance so that the chief and his people will not realize what has happened."

"And what will happen?" they asked Raven.

"Deer will have soft dry cedar bark tied behind him. When no one seems to expect it he will dance close to the day box. Then he will dip his bark into the box."

"Yes, that's a good idea," everyone said.

All was prepared. Deer was dressed in his finest dancing costume. Carefully the soft dry cedar bark was tied behind him.

When they reached the other side the dancing began. The chief and his people watched. At first there was little interest in the dancing. Then gradually Deer's dancing took hold of his audience. He danced as one inspired, inspired by the needs of his people. He danced tirelessly, drawing strength from all those who lived in darkness. Now he was by the coveted day box. Without missing a beat he dipped the dry cedar bark into the box. Instantly it caught fire. Deer started running. But the chief and his people were quicker. Before Deer could leap out of reach the fire was snuffed out.

Now the chief and his people knew that Raven wanted the daylight. The day box would be more closely guarded from now on.

Raven said, "Go and get Wren the wise one."

When Wren arrived his advice was asked. Wren said, "The chief has two beautiful daughters and the sockeye salmon are running now. Women will be cleaning and preparing fish. Turn yourselves into sockeye and swim to the other shore. When you are captured you will then have a chance to kidnap the chief's daughters."

So the people of the darkness turned themselves into sleek silvery sockeye salmon. But Raven, not wanting to be ordinary, turned himself into a huge king salmon. They swam for the other shore.

When the people of the day saw the huge king salmon among the sockeye they asked, "Is it not Raven? Yes, it must be he who wishes to take the day from us."

Again Raven and the people returned without the daylight. The people were annoyed with Raven. They grumbled. "Why couldn't Raven become a sockeye salmon like the rest of us?"

Again Wren the wise one was consulted. "The salmonberry shoots are now in season," Wren said. "The chief's daughters and the other women will be picking them. Turn yourselves into salmonberry shoots that grow on trees." The people listened and then went off on their mission.

When the chief's daughters and the other women came to pick the salmonberry shoots they were wary. They had been told to watch for any sign of trickery.

"Ohhh!" the women said. "Look at that huge, fat salmonberry shoot growing on the ground! It must be

Raven!" And away they scurried out of the bushes.

Once more the people of the darkness turned to Wren. Wren pondered deeply. This time the plan must be different. It must be a long-range plan. It must be a plan that involved something tiny instead of something big. The plan must require only one person rather than many.

"Well, what is the plan, Wren?" the people asked.

"My plan requires only one person," Wren said. "Raven must become a tiny leaf floating in the chief's spring water. When the chief's daughter comes for a drink Raven must be swallowed. Then we wait."

So it happened that Raven became a tiny leaf floating in the chief's spring water. Eventually the chief's daughter came for a drink. She blew the tiny leaves and twigs away. She drank. As she drank one tiny leaf drifted towards her mouth. Before she could stop she had swallowed it. "Oh well, it's only a leaf," she thought.

But not long after that she became pregnant. She wondered how it could have happened for she had no husband. In due time she bore a son. He was a crybaby. He cried so much that the mother and all her relatives were suspicious.

"Is it not Raven?" the old people asked. "It seems to cry too much to be one of us." But what if they were mistaken? What if the baby really belonged to the chief's daughter? They could not be sure so the baby was cared for as one of their own.

When the boy was old enough he loved to play in the canoes. He would play in them all day. The boy knew that his mother owned a paddle of great power. With one stroke the paddle could propel any canoe for a great distance. The boy began to whine for this paddle. He whined and wheedled until the mother gave in. Still, the mother was careful. The boy could have the paddle to play with but the canoe must be tied to the shore. Again the boy whined and wheedled until he was allowed to paddle freely about. The boy was watched but he did nothing unusual. Gradually, every-

one began to trust the boy. Wasn't he just a boy who liked to play like the other boys?

One day the boy began asking to play with the day box. He wanted the day box to play with in his canoe, he said. The chief would not hear of it. No, the boy must not play with the day box. The boy pleaded. He cried. Over and over he wailed, "I want to play with the day box in my canoe! I want to play with the day box in my canoe!" He got on everyone's nerves. Finally in exasperation the grandmother told the boy's mother, "You never have mercy on him. Let him play with the day box."

With the day box in his canoe the boy was watched closely the first day. But the boy did nothing wrong. He only seemed happy to play with the box in the canoe. The grandmother was satisfied.

Meanwhile Wren had sent some mice on an important mission. During the night the mice ate holes in all the canoes except that belonging to the boy.

Next morning the boy was again playing with the day box in his canoe. He was being watched but not so closely now. Then all of a sudden the boy gave a mighty thrust with his paddle. Swiftly his canoe raced over the water toward the other shore. The chief and his people panicked. They scrambled for their canoes. One by one the canoes were launched and one by one they sank helplessly. The mice had done a good job.

As the boy neared the other shore he began to uncover the day box very slowly. For the first time the people of the darkness experienced dawn. They looked and saw that it was Raven who was coming to bring them the day. It grew brighter and brighter until at last the fullness of day was upon them.

And that is the story of how we all came to have daylight.

What was Raven's reward for bringing the day? When the tide is out sometime you may notice that the ravens are the first to enjoy any food that is to be found at the water's edge. This privilege was Raven's reward.

Sechelt, 1904.

This Beautiful Country
SECHELT, 1904~1908

JOE GREGSON, AS TOLD TO HELEN DAWE

WHEN I FIRST CAME TO SECHELT to look the place over in the spring or summer of 1904 there was little here except Mr. Cook, Mr. Bert Whitaker and the Indian reservation. In 1905 I returned and went into partnership with two other men, Donelly and Newton, to operate a brickyard in Storm Bay in Sechelt Inlet. We got the clay from the Bay and used wood to fire the bricks, which were sent by scow to Vancouver. We found out, however, that the Skookumchuck [Sechelt Rapids] was a great drawback because the scows lost a day each way waiting for the tide. So we sold out in the winter of 1906–1907 to Canadian Financiers, who later went broke.

Logging was the principal industry supporting Sechelt. In 1907 I was running donkey for Sam Gray,

who had a logging camp on Sechelt Inlet. Gray's Creek, which flows into Sechelt Inlet on the mainland side, was named for him because he took up the land there as a pre-emption. Mr. Gray was in partnership with his son, also named Sam, who was hurt in the chest when a strap on a block broke loose. He died in St. Paul's Hospital about 1906, aged about forty. The father was over seventy when he died in about 1911. Mr. Gray had a daughter who married Leonard Frohlander; she died of tuberculosis.

Heaps Mills had a railroad camp at the head of Narrows Arm [Narrows Inlet], then came Gray's camp, and then one of Bert Whitaker's camps. Mr. Whitaker had two logging camps in Sechelt Inlet and a small sawmill near the Skookumchuck. There was a shingle

Interior of one of Herbert Whitaker's stores at Sechelt, c. 1913.

mill at the head of Salmon Arm [off Sechelt Inlet and south of Narrows Arm]. In 1904 logs sold for somewhere between four and six dollars a thousand board feet.

Sam Gray had a little steam tugboat, the *Reliance*, which carried freight, and I later ran the vessel for him, but I was not working on her when some of the men from the inlet camps decided to go to Vancouver to celebrate the First of July, 1907. The loggers from Heaps came down to Gray's and asked Mr. Gray if he would take them to Porpoise Bay on the *Reliance*. He told them it was all right with him if Gregson would act as engineer on the boat. They then asked me and I agreed to take them down if they would gather bark to fire up the boiler. There was plenty of bark on the beaches in those days from the many logging camps. However, gathering the bark took considerable time so that we were late leaving and arrived late in Sechelt. When we attempted to register at the hotel, the place was full and Bert Whitaker's bookkeeper charged us twenty-five cents each to sleep on the beach, even though we used our own blankets.

Mr. Whitaker sold his logging camp to Brooks, Scanlon & O'Brien in about 1906 or 1907 and I worked for this company. In 1907 or 1908 I got hurt in their camp at Narrows Arm and they paid for my expenses when I was put in hospital in Vancouver. On another occasion I was running the yarder at Narrows Arm and an engineer named Teddy Fakima was running the roader to give the logs a second start toward the water. I sent two logs down the chute together and they went out of control, knocking down a hemlock tree, which

ended up a boomstick-and-a-half distant out in the chuck, taking Fakima with it. The injured man was rowed to Porpoise Bay and transported to Sechelt, where a passing tug was chartered to take him to Vancouver. He was in St. Paul's Hospital for eleven months.

I was a witness at the test case that resulted when Fakima sued Brooks, Scanlon & O'Brien. Before this a workman found it difficult to sue his employer. They got all the tyee loggers in the country to give evidence. Fakima won the case, but the Company appealed and the decision was reversed. The case was appealed a second time, and Fakima won again.

Brooks, Scanlon & O'Brien wanted to send the case to the Privy Council but their appeal was too late. Then the Company sued for eight hundred dollars it had previously paid toward Fakima's hospital and medical bills, but the judge ruled against them because they had made the payment voluntarily. W.J. Bowser, who became Premier of BC during the First World War, was one of the lawyers for the Company. He cross-examined me at the trial.

Bert Whitaker ran the hotel in Sechelt. His first store was at Porpoise Bay, where he traded furs with the Indians. They brought him marten, mink, coon and lots of black bears. He sold the furs to his brother Ernest, who had a fur store on Water Street in Vancouver. Before I left the area Mr. Whitaker built a store in Sechelt. He owned the Porpoise Bay Wharf, a very small thing about where the present wharf is situated. There was a road past the hotel on the Sechelt waterfront over to the Porpoise Bay wharf. You could take a horse and wagon through on this road but it was not wide enough for two horses.

I remember sitting in the hotel one day when I was on my way to Vancouver. The *New Era* was coming in to the wharf with Mr. Whitaker aboard. The hotel bartender asked if anyone wanted a drink, then locked the bar and told us he was going to meet the boat. A man named John O'Brien went in through a window, opened the bar, and invited all the boys in. When Bert Whitaker arrived O'Brien asked him what kind of a bartender he had. Later in the day the bartender enquired if O'Brien still thought he was as good a man as he was before supper. O'Brien said yes, and the two men proceeded to arrange a fight in a little green place where there was a well and a windmill to raise the water. John O'Brien was beaten up, got a black eye, and it served him right.

Bert Whitaker used to take the mail up to the men in the logging camps and charged them twenty-five cents each a month whether or not they received letters. He had a fleet of boats running from Vancouver to Sechelt: the *New Era*, the *Sechelt* and the *Tartar*. After Mr Whitaker disposed of the *Sechelt* she sank off Sooke and all aboard were drowned.

I knew Captain Sam Mortimer, who was skipper of the *New Era*. I did not meet him between the time I left Sechelt and 1940, when he came aboard my boat in Granite Bay to listen to the war news on my radio. In 1906 while I was travelling to Storm Bay aboard the *New Era*, we witnessed the collision of the Canadian Pacific steamship *Princess Victoria* with the Union Steamship tug *Chehalis*. The *New Era* launched a rowboat overside, picked up perhaps four men, and put them on the *Princess Victoria*. I knew the purser of the *Chehalis*, Percy Chick, who was drowned. If the *New Era* had not been late in sailing it might have been me.

I remember two of Bert Whitaker's brothers, Ronny and Cecil. Cecil Whitaker ran a boat, the *Babine*, which plied from Porpoise Bay up Sechelt Inlet, Salmon Inlet, Jervis Inlet and Hotham Sound, carrying men and freight. The *Babine* and the *Reliance* both used the small wharf in Porpoise Bay. The water left the wharf dry sometimes at low tide, and once the *Reliance* got stuck in the mud there. I had to pull her off with a Spanish windlass.

In 1905 or 1906 two Japanese, one of them named Nakashima, started salting dog salmon (chums). They caught the fish in Sechelt Inlet, took them to their saltery at Skookumchuck, and sent the finished product to Japan and China. I believe that they were the first to put up dog salmon and they should have made a fortune. Nakashima had children and his son, called Joe, had children. The family was moved out when the Japanese were taken away from the coast during the Second World War.

The Fraser River Logging Company had a camp at Selma Park in 1907, but I never worked for the Company.

I could speak a fair amount of Chinook in those days and knew quite a number of the Sechelt Indians. Among these were Little Peter, Paul, Dominic and Chief George.

Little Peter and some Indian women were handlogging in Storm Bay. The flat near the mouth of the bay made it difficult to get the timber out and they used

Kenneth and Isobel Whitaker, c. 1913 (ages 4 and 3), standing near a wharf in front of "the Beach House," their home. The Beach House was completed in 1906.

Bert Whitaker's boat, the Tartar, c. 1910.

The Sechelt, with Trail Islands in the background, c. 1910.

a capstan to take the logs over the obstruction. The work moved at a snail's pace. The Indian women worked barefoot but some of the men wore shoes.

Fish were very plentiful and the Indians fished spring salmon with a line and jigged for cod for their own use. They did not fish commercially in the inlet because no buyers were available to take the catch. There was an Indian reservation at the Skookum-chuck, a good day's row.

Although Chief George was known as "Cultus" George, I found him reliable. He was older than I was. Once he asked me to go into partnership with him to operate a mineral claim he had. I refused because I planned to go to the Argentine. George told me "You no go," and he was right. I later met someone who knew the country and who advised me not to settle in South America. However, at the time I was talking to George I thought I wouldn't need my 'bachin' outfit when I left

"The oldest inhabitants, Sechelt, BC," 1914.

British Columbia so George purchased my cooking and sleeping equipment for five dollars. No cash changed hands then.

Quite a number of years later I was going north to run donkey. While standing at the rail of a vessel tied to the Sechelt Wharf I heard my named called several times. The person hailing me turned out to be George, who told me, "I pay now." He insisted that I go to his house, the first or second dwelling (west to east) along the tow on the reserve at that time. I thought the boat might pull out and leave me behind, but George assured me it "no go," so I went to his house and he paid me the five dollars. George was right again because I had plenty of time.

I remember the Sechelt Indian church burning down in 1906. After this the Sisters went around by boat to the logging camps to collect money to erect a new church. The Sisters also sold hospital tickets to loggers. These at first cost eight dollars a year and later the price was raised to ten dollars. The hospital tickets gave the men a bed and nursing care in St. Paul's Hospital, Vancouver, but did not provide coverage for doctors' bills or medicine. I considered that this was cheap. Loggers were not protected by Workmen's Compensation in those days.

I knew many of the men on the Union Steamship boats. Among them was Captain Bob Wilson, who came from Whitehaven, a fishing village and coal-mining town on the Cumberland coast. I had visited Whitehaven and knew Captain Wilson well. Captain Charles Moody was on the *Cassiar* for a good many years. He had "No Gambling" notices everywhere, but there was probably more gambling on that boat than on any other. I appreciated the service provided by the Union Steamships. The loggers who used the dining rooms on the boats could send their plates back for second helpings. The price of a first-class meal was about twenty-five cents in the early days. The cooks on the boats were Chinese.

I left the Sechelt area about 1908. After working at Pender Harbour I was employed, perhaps about 1910, by John Moffat to run the roader in his logging camp at Wilson Creek. Some years after I retired I returned to Sechelt and believe that I am fortunate to be living in this beautiful country.

Mr. Gregson told his recollections to Helen Dawe in February and March, 1971, when he was in his ninety-fifth year. When she had prepared a manuscript, Mr. Gregson read it carefully and indicated the necessary corrections, which have been incorporated into the article above. Joe Gregson died at Sechelt on November 1, 1971. Helen Dawe, a major historian of the Sunshine Coast, died in 1983.

the WRECK of the C.P. YORKE

Scotty McIntyre

ON DECEMBER 11, 1953, Georgia Strait was lashed by high seas and wind-driven rain with visibility down to zero. Through those conditions, the 75-foot, 100-ton tug *C.P. Yorke* was fighting her way north from her base in Vancouver with an empty rail barge in tow, headed for Beaver Cove to pick up a logging locomotive.

About eight miles northwest of Vancouver and off Buccaneer Bay, Thormanby Island, the tug was suddenly smashed down on a reef, she hit with such force that the hull was badly holed. Within minutes she had filled and her decks were awash. When the tug struck, Captain Roy Johnston managed to send a mayday on the vessel's radio, then seconds later he was washed over the side by a gigantic wave. As he started to swim he looked up and was horrified to see the barge, still under way, loom up out of the murk and crash into the tug, to which six crew men were still clinging. The barge pushed the wreck off the reef into deep water.

Meanwhile the Gulf of Georgia tug *Black Bird II*, which had been nearby, arrived in answer to the mayday. The crew plucked a semi-conscious Captain Johnston from the water, but could not locate any of the other crew men. When the scow had crashed into the tug, Chief Engineer Bill MacDonald was flung over the side but managed to grab part of a smashed lifeboat and hang on in the bitter cold for some time. Finally he had to let go, and he slipped off. He was promptly washed up on a beach, where he was later found unconscious but alive. The bodies of three crew members were found far away from each other, and two bodies were never found. The two survivors were hospitalized at Pender Harbour where they eventually recovered.

When it was decided to try to salvage the tug, the divers found her balanced on a reef in forty feet of water, and overhanging the edge of a five-hundred-foot dropoff. A ticklish situation developed, but working against time and under dangerous conditions the divers eventually managed to get slings under the vessel. Then, with the aid of two large derricks and the salvage vessel *Salvage Chief*, she was hoisted to the surface, patched up, pumped out and towed to Vancouver. She was repaired and did yeoman service for years. The *C.P. Yorke* was sold early in 1972 to Thor Larson of Weldwood Transportation, to be renamed *Trojan* and used as a private yacht.

An endnote from the aftermath of the wreck: The writer was sitting in a Vancouver coffee house recently when he was amazed to hear a folk singer perform the "Ballad of the *C.P. Yorke*." After the show I talked to the singer and he informed me that he did not know the author of the ballad, but thought it was a resident of Pender Harbour and that a record of the song had been issued and had met with moderate success.

A MATTER OF TIME

B.G. COULSON

Dedicated to the memory of Tony Fred, "Trapper," the sweetest left-handed catcher I ever knew, who died in a ridiculous logging accident. He was 41 years old.

SOMEWHERE BACK IN THE MISTY 60S, on the wildest, westest coast of British Columbia, I sweated away an entire summer on the payroll of a gyppo logging company. Any further west and the caulks would've rusted from our boot bottoms. On a clear day we could almost see Japan.

In fact, when the tide was high, our tail-blocks were actually bouncing in the goddamn water. Salt water! And the job safety breakdown didn't mention anything about seagulls on their afternoon bombing runs either.

"Hey Seymour, you take the dude in the yellow beanie, I'll get the fat guy giving signals."

Yep, it was a scene Mr. Pablo Picasso and his pal Dali would have dug immensely. Highball, V-12, tank-mounted, double-clutching, cream-the-bastard, hydraulic, screamin' jimmy, load 'n' go, rubber-tired, rock 'n' roll logging. And in the background the whitecaps of the mighty Pacific hissing softly like a blizzard of doves on blue velvet. Out there on the edge, you might say, in more ways than one.

It was the closest I ever came to actually running away and joining a circus, though it really wasn't much of a run, seeing as how my old man owned "the circus." I was a teenage kid still green as my grandmother's thumb, and wasting the holidays staggering around a sidehill, inhaling no-see-ums and pulling jaggers from my horny little hands was not high on my summer game plan. But someone had changed the game.

On the Saturday morning of the July 1st long weekend I was duly informed by The Landlord, "Son, when this holiday is over, you can start being a logger."

He made it sound like an adventure, like going camping or fishing or out to the go-kart track. Yeah, sure. Thanks, Dad. Sunday evening before my logging debut, with the rest of our family glued around Ed Sullivan and his goofy little mouse pal, I snuck down the basement stairs for a final dress rehearsal. Nine hours till showtime, and counting. . .

Slipping that huge yellow McCullogh hardhat over my ersatz Beatle cut; forcing, cursing, cramming my feet down inside those high-top Dayton leathers; a grey Stanfield nicely complementing my new Red Strap pants hooked onto my grandfather's borrowed snap suspenders—man, I figured I was primed and loaded for that mysterious world of hairy-assed BC loggers, where men are men and women ride sidesaddle. But, as Grandpa used to remind me regularly, I was just a wee bit wrong—about a whole bunch of things.

Shortly after 5:00 a.m. the next morning, I received a warning that a whole new set of rules was suddenly in place. Climbing up into the crew bus, I smiled at the driver whom I'd known forever and said, "Good mornin', Bob!"

"Oh, I doubt that very goddamn much," he muttered, lurching the bus away in first gear sending me balls over bootlaces down the aisle toward that place traditionally reserved for the boss's son—the very back seat. "Welcome to the wonderful world of logging, Slick. Staying long?"

See, back in those days, the social hierarchy of a one-side gyppo logging show had little to do with seniority and even less to do with registered birthright. The pecking order of a woods crew put the equipment operators at the very top, the hooktender close behind, then the rigging rats, next the native Indians, and finally anyone directly related to The Boss. Obviously my best chance for survival lay in hooking up with the Indian guys. So I did, almost as if I knew what I was doing.

Now referred to as "The Summer of Love," that month of July, 1967 was, as an old donkey-puncher amigo used to say, the longest three years of my life. Because a body needed to work thirty consecutive calendar days before being officially accepted into the almighty IWA, anyone who could not or would not pack his own weight was quickly canned or chunked out. Or, in the plainest available English even a part-time moron could understand, "Your sad ass is fired, Jack!" With the crew serenading off-key in the background, "Yer leavin'...on a floatplane..."

Once you were in The Union, however, you immediately acquired certain rights which your employer had to honour, but up till then you were just another name in the rain, "and lots more where you came from, pal, so if yer gonna fall, fall towards the riggin' cuz we come to log, not fuck the dog!" And the beauty of working with native boys was the way they'd automatically treat you like a good guy, at least till you proved otherwise.

Nobody aimed a word in my direction that first morning until we were all standing around the foreman's pickup, sipping coffee, waiting while the giant engines of the Tyee yarder and Skagit log loader warmed up slowly, electric dinosaurs throbbing in the background. Finally one of the fallers, Shorty McLean, a guy with a perpetual "hate-on" for the world, said to the bull-bucker, "Whaddya think, Bill, should we piss on this punk, make 'im smell like a man?"

I didn't need a program to know I was their intended target. Then a very large native rigging-slinger said to me, "So what's your job here gonna be, partner?"

"I think I'm supposed to set the chokers," I told him, trying to sound like I even knew what that meant. He stared blankly at me while the rest of the crew looked away trying not to laugh, shuffling feet and biting lips in the damp dawn chill.

"Well, that's a pretty good place to start," he said, "so tell me, where you got your choker hidden?" Dead silence, except for the odd snicker. How could my dad forget to tell me I needed to bring a choker, whatever they were, for Christ's sake? This was not a great launch for my logging career. I began perspiring in all the wrong places. Places it wouldn't be cool to scratch.

"Aww, don't worry, kid, you can borrow mine today, just don't break it, 'cause it's my favourite one." He took off his battered orange hardhat and conked it down on top of mine, punctuating what he'd just said, though not too hard, and then he winked right at me while the rest of the crew tried not to wet themselves laughing.

I had just survived my first head-on encounter with the great "Ray Seecher, the chokerman's teacher," as he liked to introduce himself. And as things turned out, the lessons he was dealing were definitely not available from any books or night-school courses. This guy was straight goods.

"This is my cousin, Charlie Jack," Ray said, after the others had all disappeared in various directions, some clambering up into machines. A wiry little guy with a gap-toothed grin held out his hand.

"How now, partner!" he chuckled.

Then Ray pointed up the mountainside, where a thousand logs lay scattered across each other like a giant game of Pick-up Sticks. "That's where we work, kid," he said. "Follow me." And then he was off. Off like the bride's pajamas, as the saying goes. Fast.

They've got me confused with a frigging mountain goat, was my first thought halfway up the hillside where I'd paused to deposit my breakfast. Through my upchucking I heard Charlie yell, "Hey, Ray, we must be logging up a bit too high. This young fella is airsick already."

Eventually, after fifteen minutes of climbing over stacks of jumbled logs and tumbling face-first a dozen times down into hidden pockets of branch-covered holes in the slash, I finally caught up with the guys at the back end. I felt like I'd been caught in a cat-scrap. From our new vantage point we could see for miles in every direction. Rolling valleys carpeted with dazzling green rugs of forest, small lakes glistening in the sun's morning rays—calendar shots whichever way you looked. A million-dollar view right out of a beer commercial, and it all came free with the job.

Then the serenity of the postcard scene below us was rudely fractured by a jangle of the cold steel butt-rigging. It danced and clanged back to where we waited perched like a trio of beavers on a giant downed red cedar. "Bing bing KLANGGG...Bing bing bing...KERRANGGG."

With his right hand, Ray squeezed the two trigger buttons on "the bug"—the electronic radio-signal transmitter slung low around his waist, and with a screaming "BEEEEEEEEEEP" echoing between the mountains, all sound and motion came to a slow, grinding halt.

"See that?" Ray asked, pointing to the three long cables dangling in the air, a dull orange blob of steel attached to each one. "The new baby on the front is mine, the middle one is cousin Chuck's, and that curly one on the back from the museum is yours. That's the rules, partner, new guy gets the back bead. Pull hard, she comes easy!"

By the time Ray had shown me a couple of times how to slide the bell up the choker, throw the knob end across the log, reach underneath and lock the knob into the hole in the bell collar to cinch it up tight like a necktie, the novelty of being a chokerman had worn off. Soon I was wondering out loud when it was time for coffee break.

"We don't give chokermen coffee breaks," Ray laughed, "too hard to re-train 'em."

For some reason, I didn't mind their gentle abuse. Twisted or not, it still felt like an olive branch to me. Later, whenever I'd be yanking my choker through the woods and it would snag on a limb or tangle up in the brush, big Ray would yell, "Better pull harder, kid, you're hung up on a leaf."

If I somehow "mollied" the pin for the haulback block in backwards, or was the last guy getting into the clear before he could blow "GO AHEAD" on the turn, or sometimes when he just felt like making conversation, Ray would stare at me and ask, "This is your first day in the woods, sonny?" But always with the hint of a smile. Whenever a turn was snorting toward the landing and my snare came undone, or the log slipped out of my bead causing a dog-cock, Charlie would offer the gentle reminder, "Relax, partner, we couldn't fire you even if we wanted to."

They used to ask me at least twice a week, "So tell us what you did to your old man that made him give you this wonderful job. It must've been something real terrible!"

At day's end we'd all race down the hill and stumble into the landing, and old Oil Spill Bill, the mechanic, would shake his head and say, "Man, you three are quite a pair." I don't know about the Indian guys, but I kind of liked it.

Now all summer long Charlie had been showing me how he could tell the time by using only his arms and the sun, kind of like a human sundial. Whenever the morning seemed to be dragging—pretty well every bloody day—I'd ask Charlie what time he thought it was, and if the sun was even partially shining, he'd go into his well-rehearsed routine. First, he'd climb to a spot up above me on the hill. Then he'd gaze directly into the sun for ten seconds or so, whip off his dented blue hardhat, and hold it out at arm's length to block the glare. Next, he'd lift his other arm straight away from his shoulder, casting a shadow on the ground beside him. After studying this awhile, he'd raise one leg up slowly behind him and announce in the world's worst John Wayne imitation, "It's exactly twenty-seven minutes after ten o'clock a.m. in the morning, Pacific Charlie Time, approximately."

So then we'd blow "a long and a short" signal on the radio whistle, "BEEEEEEEEEEEEP, BEEP," which meant all machines in the landing got shut down immediately, to allow the rigging crew to communicate down the hill.

"What the hell d'ya want now?" the low-life chaser would yell up the hillside, once everything got quiet.

"What time is it, white trash?" I'd holler back. We could see him asking Joe, the grapple operator.

"It's almost ten-thirty, ya faggot!" the chaser would scream up at us as the machines roared back to life.

"They're three minutes out down there, that guy must have a Timex," Charlie would say in his laid-back drawl.

Ray would just chuckle, "Relax partner, we can always split the difference."

Needless to say I was heavily impressed the first time they performed this act. As I was every time they pulled it on me—sometimes twice a day when they were feeling frisky. I could not believe how this shaman-logger and his hokus-pokus came within a few minutes of a real clock every damn time! Soon I was raving about my pal Charlie's special talent to anyone who would listen.

When I'd ask Charlie to share the secret, his reply was always the same. "Partner, I'll explain it so even a white boy son-of-the-boss can understand. It's kind of like . . . magic!"

This little charade went on till the last Thursday of my last week, or "Weekend Eve," as my brown-skinned buddies called Thursday afternoons. Finally I broke down.

"Name your price," I pleaded. Ray and Charlie started jumping around, waving their arms and war-whooping in a victory dance, howling with a P.T. Barnum "sucker born every minute" kind of glee. The bait was on the hook, the fish was in the mood; it was nolo contendere, Your Honour. And those merry pranksters were digging their little joke to the max.

"Just a matter of time, partner," Charlie chortled.

"Aw, c'mon, you guys," I said, thinking I was close to learning the all-time parlour trick that would help me through college, maybe even to an early retirement.

"Well son," Charlie said, putting his arm around my shoulder, "I guess the real secret is . . . the heat."

By now I was in the net, hell, I was almost in the boat.

"The heat?" I asked, trying not to sound too much like a city kid, let alone a Size 12 idiot.

"Yeah, the heat," Charlie said, "'cause if you don't get enough heat on the solder, then the damn thing don't stick!" By now Ray was having a shit-fit, laughing hard enough for three men. In slow motion, Charlie took off his hardhat and held it at arm's length, with the inside facing us. "Took me about three tries before I finally got that sonofagun to stay in there."

For the longest time I just stood beside him, staring at the ancient pocket watch stuck to the inside of Charlie's tin lid. The damn thing even had a sweep hand. I felt him squeeze my shoulder twice, ever so gently. "Gotcha, rook!"

Ray said later he was going to send in an accident report to the Workers' Compensation Board that said: "Broke two ribs and peed myself, while laughing at boss's kid."

The next evening after work, Ray and Charlie invited me to get off the crummy with them and have a beer down by the river to celebrate my last day on the job. "We've got a real nice reservation for you," was the way Ray put it.

What could I do, seeing as how there was no counter-offer forthcoming from the whiter shade of crew?

So there we were, the three of us, sipping brown barley on the Indian side of the Somass River, when Charlie finally spoke. "Hey partner, you remember that little trick I been showing you? We'll I'd sure appreciate it if you kept it, you know, kind of . . . under your hat!"

Yesterday I went to Charlie's funeral up on the reserve. Later, at the wake, a beautiful young girl about sixteen, with Ray's sad deep eyes and straight, shiny black hair swinging down to her waist came across the longhouse floor to offer me a tray of sweets. "Did you know my uncle Charlie?" she asked.

I smiled at her and reached for a square of Nanaimo bar.

"Yes, I guess I did . . . a long time ago," I said. Her bottom lip was trembling, and I noticed that she had tucked a well used hankie in the sleeve of her dress.

"Did you know him quite well?" she asked softly.

"Young lady," I told her, "Back when I was about the same age you are right now, your uncle Charlie and your father taught me how to tell time . . . the Indian way."

Driving home from across the river last night, I was wishing I could've told her some of the other stuff those Indian boys taught me, way back there in the Summer of Love, when the three of us had jobs in "the circus."

But on the other hand, maybe sometimes a guy is better off keeping certain things under his hat. I miss ya, partner. Thanks for the time.